HARRIET MONROE

By DANIEL J. CAHILL

University of Northern Iowa

D0103437

Twayne Publishers :: New York

For My Father and Mother

Preface

Literary historians have honored *Poetry: A Magazine of Verse* and have accorded it a permanent place in the shaping forces of modern poetry. The abundant richness of this modern movement might well have been less spectacular without the encouragement and vitality which *Poetry* offered in those years when the young poets were seeking to break the bonds of traditionalism and to create a new poetic voice for the modern age. This renaissance of poetic literature owes an enormous debt to Harriet Monroe, the founder-editor of *Poetry: A Magazine of Verse*. This present study is, in part, an attempt to assess the value of her contribution to the larger movement of modern poetry.

Some literary figures are important because of the special excellence of their works; others, because of the crucial role they played in the encouragement of literature. Surely, Ezra Pound is a memorable example of this dual role for a man of letters; and Harriet Monroe merits a similar position. Although a minor poet of considerable grace, her editorial efforts to serve the cause of poetry not only eclipse the quality of her works but also assure her a permanent place in the history of modern poetry. Aware of the dangers of her venture, she had the courage and determination to found a magazine devoted exclusively to poetry. Although she modestly hoped that her magazine would live for five years, the future greatness which it later achieved was a great source of pride for Miss Monroe. In a time when poetry was only accorded the status of "page-filler" in the larger commercial journals, she gave the poet an opportunity and a place for a serious hearing. In a world which refused "to conceive of poetry high enough," she was determined to encourage the poet to speak with the authoritative voice of his art.

My main objective of this study has been to present the work of Harriet Monroe and to give a balanced analysis of her unique contribution to the present state of modern poetry. Her efforts have been abundantly praised and attacked by poets and critics alike; but, in a career as long and complex as hers, it is inevitable that we find failure mixed with much success. As a poet, she produced a body of charming, perceptive, lyrical poetry which still deserves the attention accorded to a good minor poet. In her own poetry, she tried to strike a contemporary note in form and in subject matter. In this sense, she was an experimental poet. Her poetry may seem less radical today because much of the catholicity that she brought to her work has become part of the vital fabric of modern poetry. Nevertheless, her poetry can be appreciated for its firmness and clarity, as well as for its energy and seriousness. Her contribution of work to the great fund of American poetry is the voice of a limited and minor poet, but hers is still a quiet one of assurance that speaks of the grandeur of man's hopes and achievements. Her poetic record celebrates life's smaller triumphs of rare and true understanding, of life as a blessing and not as a curse.

Since almost all of Miss Monroe's poetry is out of print and since few readers are familiar with more than a few of her poems, I have quoted a number of them in full. I hope, by quoting freely and at length, to convey some of the feeling which she had for modern poetry. Miss Monroe frequently drew her inspiration for poetry from the modern scene, and she hoped that other poets would see the same vitality in the modern mechanized world. She viewed the Age of the Machine as genuinely progressive because, in her mind, it opened new wonders and new possibilities for man's conquest of his environment. In addition to these many poems, we find also a more private and lyrical strain—works which owe their excellence to the poetic insights into the glory and pain of life.

In her more considerable role as editor, Miss Monroe has been attacked because—as some of her more adverse critics maintained—hers was not a truly revolutionary spirit: she was too catholic in poetic taste and judgment. In one perspective, these charges are not without substance. On the other hand, few critics have denied the significance of her role as editor in discovering and in fostering the best talents of modern poetry. Miss Monroe was among the first to give sympathetic encourage-

Preface

ment to Vachel Lindsay, Rupert Brooke, Elinor Wylie, Louise Bogan, Marianne Moore, Robinson Jeffers, Stephen Spender, and Hart Crane. In this study, I have preferred to present this more positive side of her contribution to literature—both as a poet and as an editor.

I undertook writing this book because it seemed to me that, in the full sweep of the Twayne Series, Harriet Monroe had a place of historical significance to the student of literature. Inevitably, the emergence of modern poetry returns again and again to the pages of *Poetry* and to its founder-editor who had the insight and critical judgment to bring serious poets before the public. Miss Monroe fully believed Walt Whitman's famous dicta that, in order to have great poets, one must also have a great audience. How closely that ideal has been approached through the pages of *Poetry* is an essential part of this book. The history of *Poetry* under Harriet Monroe is a central part of this study because it represents, in large measure, the history and success of American poetry. Surely today there is a greater and more sensitive audience, one more willing to accord the poet a serious place in modern literature. As a poet and editor, Harriet Monroe was responsible for shaping this larger, more sympathetic audience.

I am pleased to record the names of my colleagues who generously gave me their encouragement and assistance in preparing this volume: Dudley Flamm, who saved me from some of my worst excesses of style; and Richard Fehner, who charmed me into greater clarity when I had already rested satisfied. I will always owe more honor than I can repay to Frederick P. W. McDowell of the University of Iowa: he has been a generous friend and critic. No work of any length can come into being without the quiet encouragement of one's wife; and I gratefully acknowledge the charming persistence of my wife, Karma, as she helped me through many stages of this book.

I also wish to thank the librarians and curators of the Harriet Monroe Collection at the University of Chicago Library. They generously allowed me to examine the many letters and documents pertaining to *Poetry* which Miss Monroe left to the University of Chicago upon her death in 1936. Special thanks are due to President Sidney Rand of St. Olaf College for granting financial assistance to bring my work to completion.

The Macmillan Company has kindly given me permission to quote from various collections of Harriet Monroe's poetry.

DANIEL J. CAHILL

University of Northern Iowa
Cedar Falls, Iowa

Contents

Chronology

1860   Harriet Monroe born December 23 in Chicago, Illinois.

1867   Attended Moseley School, Chicago.

1877   Educated at Visitation Convent in Georgetown.

1880's An effort to gain a modest start in the world of journalism. Active in the Fortnightly, a literary group.

1888   Living in New York. Drama critic for the *New York Herald Tribune*. Made many new friends in the bohemian world of artists and writers. Returned to Chicago late in 1889.

1889   Wrote an ode for the dedication of Chicago's New Auditorium.

1890   Accepted the position of art critic for the *Chicago Tribune*. Made her first European tour and met many prominent literary figures in England.

1892   First published work—*Valeria and Other Poems*—printed as a private edition. Wrote the "Columbian Ode" for the dedication of the Columbian Exposition, 1892-93.

1893   Free-lance journalist for the *Chicago Times-Herald*.

1894   Trial for damages against the *New York World* for unauthorized printing of the "Columbian Ode."

1896   Published *John Wellborn Root*, a memoir of her brother-in-law, famed architect of the Columbian Exposition.

1897   Second European tour. Traveled about the Continent for one year; again met many of the significant literary figures of the time.

1898   Returned to Chicago. Continued to submit poetry to the literary journals with little success of publication. Some poems appeared in *Atlantic* and London's *Fortnightly Review*.

1901   Journey to the Western states.

1903   Published *The Passing Show*, collection of plays written between 1885 and 1900.

1906   Worked on a series of prose plays, but never received the encouragement of a dramatic production.

1900- Continued to submit poems to various literary journals and
1912   to support herself meagerly with sporadic jobs in free-lance journalism.

1909   Resumed the position of art critic for *Chicago Tribune*, a post which she held for five years.

1911   The founding and planning of *Poetry: A Magazine of Verse,* a venture which grew partly from personal frustration at the closed-door policy of editors toward new serious poets. Monroe retained her position as founder-editor until her death in 1936.

1912   First issue of *Poetry* published, September 23.

1914   Published *You and I,* collection of poems.

1917   *The New Poetry: An Anthology of Twentieth Century Verse in English,* edited by Harriet Monroe and Alice Corbin Henderson.

1923   Published a new enlarged and revised edition of *The New Poetry: An Anthology.* Third European tour.

1924   *The Difference and Other Poems.*

1926   *Poets and Their Art: A Collection of Essays.*

1932   Published new revised edition of *The New Poetry* and *Poets and Their Times.*

1933   Long tour in Mexico.

1934   Second journey to the Orient.

1935   Started to write her autobiography.

1936   Attended the International Association of Poets, Playwrights, Editors, Essayists, and Novelists Conference in Buenos Aires. Died in Peru, September 26, 1936, on her return journey to the United States. Buried in Arequipa, Peru.

1938   Posthumous publication of her autobiography, *A Poet's Life: Seventy Years in a Changing World.*

CHAPTER 1

Youthful Aspirations

I *The Early Years*

HARRIET Monroe was a born Chicagoan, and her life-long affection and enthusiasm for the city of her youth was one of the most stable attitudes of her life. Born December 23, 1860, she witnessed the decades of struggle as Chicago fought for recognition as a great industrial and cultural center of America. The vast record of Chicago's growth as a giant urban center of immense wealth and influence has—in the life of Harriet Monroe—a parallel history in which she gave shape to her achievements. In later years, when Miss Monroe founded *Poetry*, she was keenly aware of her Midwest heritage; she was consciously attempting to give voice to the claims of a general culture and substance to the poetic renaissance in mid-America. As an editor, her single-handed efforts were prophetic in stirring the latent talents of the Midwest and in shaping a movement in verse that was both modern and revolutionary. She had hoped to achieve some of the dynamism and excitement of her native city for poetry and to win for the Midwest a sense of recognition as a true center of culture. The role she played in the Chicago literary renaissance is considerable, and it has won for her a permanent place in American literary history. Miss Monroe's contribution to twentieth-century poetry—both as poet and as editor—are the subjects of this study.

Harriet Monroe was the second of four children whose parents, Henry Stanton Monroe and Martha Monroe, were people of moderately wealthy means who had come to Chicago in the early 1850's. The son of a New York lawyer, Henry Monroe had left the East early in 1852 to establish a law firm in the new city of the Midwest. With its aura of frontier enthusiasm, Chicago must have seemed to Henry Monroe a place of great opportunity for a young lawyer. The sophisticated easterner soon fell in love with the new city, and a promising future seemed assured. Within a short time, he asked Martha Mitchell to share that future with him. Scotch by ancestry, Martha was an orphan who had come to Chicago from Akron, Ohio, to live with two spinster aunts; she was a girl of great charm and beauty. After a brief courtship, Henry Monroe and Martha were married in 1855. Two years later, their first child, Dora Louise, joined the young family. The second child, Harriet, was born three years later; her birth was followed by that of two other children: a daughter, Lucy; a son, William Stanton.

In her autobiography, A Poet's Life, Harriet Monroe conveys an affectionate and sympathetic portraiture of her family life. She is tenderly candid in exploring the memories of people and events which influenced and gave shape to her character. Her early family life was not always one of serenity, and in certain respects it might even be considered an unhappy one. Her father, a man of some erudition and social grace, had married a woman who, though beautiful, was socially awkward and possessed of little intellectual polish. Young and ambitious for a place in the professional and social world, Henry Monroe found his wife to be a quiet and more retiring woman than the image of success demanded.

In spirit, Mr. Monroe was the antithesis of his wife. He was fired with a love of learning and with a strong desire for an active social life, which to a man in his position was almost a requisite. But his wife, who felt no yearning to expand her personality, was content to perform the simple duties of a devoted wife and loving mother; and her inability to cope with the tensions which arose from this difference of personalities was understandable: there was nothing in her experience to prepare her for the situation. In spite of these tensions, Harriet's mother was a woman who cared very deeply for the love and affection of her family. From her mother, Harriet inherited a great sense of kindness and personal loyalty in her associations with people, as well as a good portion of her mother's beauty.

From her father, Miss Monroe gained her love for a life of learning and an appreciation of the arts. As a young girl, she idolized her father; and the bond of sympathy which grew between them gave strength to her early desires for a life

devoted to literature. She found the keenest enjoyment in read-
ing books from her father's large library; and, like Virginia
Woolf, it might be said that she was educated in her father's
library. Mr. Monroe's interests in the arts also extended beyond
the literary into the fields of painting and music; and, with
her father's encouragement, Harriet acquired an extensive
knowledge of these two arts, one which she later found useful
as the art and music critic for the *Chicago Tribune*. The entire
emphasis of her father's influence was along artistic lines, and
it strongly marked her life. It might be said also that she
acquired some of his legalistic acuteness in attacking and solving
problems.

After the great Chicago Fire of 1871, Mr. Monroe suffered
financial reverses because of unfortunate business associations;
and, while the early years of his marriage were satisfying ones, the
strain of losing both his social and financial status proved dis-
astrous to his marital happiness. In a sense, the Monroes were,
as we have noted, incompatible because the family was the
whole of Mrs. Monroe's existence; Mr. Monroe, on the other hand,
required a more active life. In an effort to achieve some form
of inner life which transcended the routine cares of the family,
Harriet's father became more dependent on the solitude of his
library; and, by degrees, his affection for family life disappeared.
This reclusive tendency was no asset to his professional career,
which soon began to suffer from inattention. He found it more
and more difficult to live up to the promise of his early dreams
when he had first settled in Chicago.

Of her parents, Miss Monroe wrote that they "lived more or
less at cross purposes, neither understanding nor deferring to
the other"; but, although the basic personality conflicts of her
parents have been stated in a concise and stark manner, it would
be a distortion of the true situation to conclude that these ten-
sions were always present. Nonetheless, the tensions of her
family environment were reflected in the child Harriet's responses
to life. A shy and inhibited girl, she allowed herself to submit
to the childishly cruel domination of her elder sister. Harriet,
never robust, suffered in her youth from a chronic nervousness
that at various times threatened to undermine her health. Gen-
erally frail and sickly in youth, she was always acutely sensitive
to her own feelings and a keen observer of those of others.

Harriet Monroe's formal education was limited not only by
family finances but, more importantly, by the conventional atti-
tudes of the times concerning the role of the female in society.
Her elementary education was acquired in the Moseley Public
Grammar School, and at the age of twelve she attended Dear-
born Seminary. Five years later, in 1877, she enrolled at Visitation
Convent in Georgetown; she was graduated from this school in
1879. Under the direction of the nuns at Visitation, her education
comprised the usual studies of Victorian female seminaries; but
the environment of the school smoothed the rough edges of her
temperamental personality. The "fine lady" tradition of Visitation
permanently affected her character; and, of course, it had an
ultimate affect on *Poetry*—a point which often irritated Ezra
Pound during his early association with the magazine: "There
was little of the dilettante in Miss Monroe's personality. Her
judgment was thoroughly grounded in a liberal, humanized
education."[1]

While attending Visitation, Miss Monroe acquired a sense
of independence and self-sufficiency; and the encouragement
which the nuns extended to Harriet's literary aspirations gave
strength and substance to her ambitions. The convent school
also proved advantageous for Harriet socially, for she formed
many lasting friendships with the daughters of wealthy and
influential easterners. These fortuitous friendships helped to
wean Miss Monroe from her protective covering of shy reticence
and to make her more socially oriented. Her former acquiescence
in social relations and her quiet submission to events were now
supplanted by a more active and radical outlook, but this new
attitude proved not to be the mere radicalism of youth. Miss
Monroe was possessed of a strong sense of personal value and
integrity, and in this spirit of confidence, she was eager for
change. This attitude was definitely an enduring cast of mind
which followed her into maturity and became part of her habitual
response to life.

When Harriet Monroe recorded the memories of her child-
hood and youth in her autobiography, she was intent upon
unfolding those events and influences which informed her mature
judgment and character. On almost every page of the book,
there is the impress of her father's charm and intellectual cast.
The influence of her education made a special mark upon her

mind and personality, and the kind of education available to young ladies before the turn of the century stressed a very genteel tradition and the role of family life. Although she absorbed many of the patterns of the feminine social image, she also possessed a fine sense of intellectual independence. In later years, when she was pressed by difficult financial circumstances, she never wavered in her determination to find solutions to them. Eager for new adventures and dedicated to the power of poetry to breathe freshness into life, she never accepted defeat. As influences, the forces of her family and school life help explain the character of her own poetry and also the kind of able editorship that she provided for her magazine.

Although she was for a time educated in a convent school, Miss Monroe was strangely indifferent to the powers of religion, and supernatural theism played no important role in her philosophic attitudes. She was not a religious person either by training or by inclination. Indeed, the whole attitude of the Monroe family toward religion was one of puzzlement and indifference, and attendance at church was always an event of minor significance for them. Of her own religious convictions, Miss Monroe wrote: "Gradually I lost entirely all allegiance to the old creeds."[2] In summing up her philosophy of life, she wrote the following statement several weeks before her death in 1936:

No doubt I must confess myself a heathen. If religion means allegiance to any sect or church . . . then I am completely irreligious. . . . But I am a quite untroubled heathen. For me the important issues have concerned this life on earth, not the theoretic next one in some ritualized Heaven or realistic Hell. . . . The mystery is not the greatness of life, but its littleness. That we, so grandly born, so mightily endowed, should grope with blind eyes and bound limbs in the dust and mire of petty desires and grievances; until we can hardly see the blue of the sky or the glory of the seasons, until we can hardly clasp our neighbor's hand or hear his voice—this is the inexplicable mystery, the blasting unreality, the bitter falsehood that underlies all the dark evils of the world.[3]

Frederick J. Hoffman has aptly characterized Miss Monroe as a liberal humanist, as a woman with her faith grounded upon man's potential for a greater human perfection and worldly progress. Indeed, she looked with eager vision to the future, to a brighter epoch when man's capacity for distrust and hatred was eclipsed by his innate power for love and community. She always viewed life in these affirmative terms, and her poetry reflects this sense of optimism, one darkened only intermittently with distress for man's selfishness.

The interim between the completion of her formal education in 1879 and the founding of *Poetry* in 1912 was one of intense activity: writing, traveling, lecturing, teaching, and enjoying a host of other pursuits, both professional and social. These were years filled with aspirations, events, and some minor successes; but basically they constitute a period of false starts in poetic drama and a kind of genteel free-lance reviewing and journalistic criticism.

After graduation from Visitation, Miss Monroe returned to the home of her father, where she remained until his death in 1903. It was not the social convention of the time for a young woman of her class to be employed, and the idea of a career was not yet considered respectable. The general attitude of the 1890's was that, in the normal course of events, a young girl would marry and establish a home of her own; but, in the case of Miss Monroe, events did not proceed in the planned order. In her autobiography, she admitted that she had never felt a strong inclination toward marriage. Perhaps she was too independent of mind or could not imagine herself bound to a life condition which imposed so many restrictions upon her personal freedom. For a woman of her intellectual aspirations, she simply preferred the single life.

The years between 1880 and 1888 were searching years for Harriet; she tried her hand at a number of minor journalistic ventures and at some more serious literary writing. In 1880, when Harriet traveled to New York for an extended vacation, her increasing circle of new friends proved advantageous; and, along with her interest in journalism, they helped to open a number of opportunities that might have otherwise remained closed to her. While in New York, she quickly became acquainted with many of the commanding figures in the journalistic and literary circles; and among these were Margaret Sullivan and Eugene Field. Through Field, Harriet was introduced to Edmund C. Stedman, who was then the most important literary figure in New York.

As a result of her Sunday evening visits to Stedman's home, she first met such people as Robert L. Stevenson, William Dean Howells, and Frank R. Stockton, who later helped and encouraged her in her literary endeavors. "The evenings at Stedman's house in Bronxville were of a kind that supplied fuel to her later activities . . . and from Stedman himself Harriet Monroe perhaps caught fire, from his prophetic fervor and belief in the future of American poetry."[4] This close contact with people of literary achievement gave impetus to Harriet's "grandiloquent literary aspirations," as she dubbed them in retrospect. Her entire stay in New York was, therefore, advantageous both professionally and socially; for she widened her circle of friends to include many influential people who were later to prove themselves loyal in the receptive spirit which they extended toward *Poetry*.

The year 1889 was one of special achievement for Miss Monroe. Her first published poem, "With a Copy of Shelley," appeared in *The Century*, one of the major periodicals of the time; and the encouragement of that event renewed her efforts to seek a larger forum for poetry. In the summer of the same year, she also wrote and revised a verse tragedy, *Valeria*. Because of her emerging interest in drama, her poetic energies were temporarily invested in such verse, and she worked on a number of plays which expressed her preoccupation with modern themes. During this period, Miss Monroe experimented with a variety of dramatic forms in which she employed the measured language of poetry, and she attempted to harmonize realism of subject with the power of verse. In addition to her dramatic experiments, she was also engaged at various intervals as a correspondent for the *Chicago Tribune*. As a free-lance journalist, she wrote a number of feature columns in which she reviewed many of the major art exhibits and musical events. Through her literary and critical activities, she was deeply engaged in the cultural world of Chicago, and she was constantly expanding her acquaintanceship and influence among that group of people who were attempting to find a more appreciative and extensive audience for art in Chicago.

The first of many voyages, Miss Monroe made her tour abroad in 1890, visiting France, Italy, and England. While in London, she stayed with Mr. and Mrs. Henry Harland, friends whom

she had met in New York at the Stedmans'. As founder-editor
of *The Yellow Book*, Henry Harland was intimately connected
with the avant-garde writers of the 1890's; and, as a matter of
friendship, he introduced Harriet Monroe to many of the leading
literary figures of the time. In her autobiography, Harriet re-
counted fascinating conversations with Henry James, Aubrey
Beardsley, James McNeill Whistler, and others. She gained a
sense of the stir and movement of radical ideas in literature
and painting; however, if we accept her autobiographical com-
ments, she seemed singularly unalert to much of the distin-
guished—if minor—poetry that was being written in the period.
Certainly, Miss Monroe did not exhibit any depth of under-
standing for the Esthetic movement or even for the radical
pessimism of Thomas Hardy. In all events, she would probably
not have approved of the philosophical tone of the 1890's since
her midwestern mind was closed to the ideas and innovations
of *The Yellow Book*. Nonetheless, her connections with Henry
Harland and his literary cohorts were valuable because they
expanded her acquaintanceship with a literary tradition and
with a number of forefront poets who later proved helpful in
the early days of *Poetry*.

This first European journey was a highly invigorating ex-
perience for Miss Monroe. Spending a major portion of her
time in London, she toured the great art galleries of England;
and, when her travels took her to France and Italy, she broad-
ened her experiences in the plastic arts by viewing the works
of the masters of those countries. For Miss Monroe, the critical
appreciation of painting was more than the casual effort of
an amateur traveler trying to absorb the culture of Europe.
She had an exceedingly critical eye for good art; indeed, paint-
ing was her second major preoccupation.

When Harriet returned to Chicago in December, 1890, plans
for the establishment of the Chicago Art Institute were being
formulated. The new institute was a tremendous adventure
for citizens of Chicago, and its final completion solidified the
city's position as an important cultural center of the Midwest.
Spacious and beautiful, the new art gallery attracted international
attention; and the institute's now famous collection of the French
Impressionists was acquired in those early stimulating decades.
During these energizing years in the art world, Harriet Monroe

had resumed her career as art critic for the *Chicago Tribune,* and in that capacity her commentaries on art ranged widely over the works of such artists as Saint-Gaudens, George Bellows, Augustus John, Albert Pinkham Ryder, Paul Gauguin, Paul Cézanne, Vincent Van Gogh, and many others. Miss Monroe's journalistic art essays of this period in her life suggest a wide range of appreciations and a ready knowledge of the traditions and innovations of painting. Many of these articles display a genuine flair for sharp analysis of technique and a quick appreciation for form and precision of lines. Occasionally Miss Monroe's bias for the American artist came to the foreground, as it later did as editor of *Poetry.*

Despite her qualifications as an art critic, Miss Monroe was relieved of her position in less than six months because the *Tribune* discovered that Harriet's young sister, Lucy, was writing a similar column for a rival paper, the *Herald.* Irrational as it may seem today, the *Tribune's* policy would not allow such a situation to continue. And, since it was impossible to secure a similar journalistic position, Miss Monroe was forced to eke out a meager living by sporadic magazine writing, a little teaching, and some lecturing. Such was the general pattern of her financial resources for almost the next twenty years.

In 1890, Harriet had achieved a degree of local acclaim by writing a dedication ode for Chicago's new auditorium. The "Ode," a highly academic work, is a frank hymn to her native city. The motive which prompted her to offer her poem was the distressing feeling that the arts of music, painting, and architecture were frequently being awarded an integral place in public life while poetry was neglected and relegated to the status of being a page-filler in magazines. The auditorium "Ode" set the stage, moreover, for a more ambitious project for Miss Monroe.

II   *The Columbian Exposition*

Early in 1890, Chicago had been selected as the site of the Columbian Exposition, a great celebration to mark the four-hundredth anniversary of the discovery of America. The exposition was an event of international importance, and the fact that Chicago became the chosen site indicated the cultural and

industrial achievements taking place in the Midwest. The pur-
pose of the exposition was, of course, to stimulate world interest
in Chicago as a progressive business center, but the planners
of the great fair did not permit the commercial aspect to over-
shadow the advance that the city had achieved in the arts. The
prepared program of the fair was designed to stress Chicago
as a new cultural center, and the arts of painting, music, sculp-
ture, and architecture were to play a prominent role in the
exposition.

The Columbian Exposition is now local history, and the vision
and hopes of its planners have receded into minor importance,
but the exposition consumed the talents of many people—Daniel
Burnham, Louis Sullivan, John W. Root, to name only a few.
The grandiloquent plans for the architecture of the fair were
centered on making the exposition a world-renowned showcase
of design; and, since the emphasis was to be on beauty, the
chosen site in Jackson Park was ideally suited to the scope
of the plans. From the very beginning, the plans for the fair
were an intimate part of the Monroe family's conversation; for
John Wellborn Root, a young architect of talent and one of the
initial planners of the fair, was also Harriet's brother-in-law.
Miss Monroe's respect and admiration for Root may be seen
in the personal memoir which she published after his death
in 1896.

Perhaps because of Root's influence, perhaps because she
loved poetry, Harriet became dissatisfied that no plans for
honoring poetry were considered by the committee of affairs
for the exposition, although architecture, painting, and music
were to be honored. Since one of the expressed purposes of
the fair was to promote the arts and thereby to display the
cultural advantages of the country and since no one seemed
to speak for poetry, Harriet determined that the task must fall
to her. With a characteristic bravery, she offered her services
as a poet to the fair's committee on ceremonies. To her surprise,
the committee accepted her proposal to write a dedicatory ode
for the exposition.

Harriet worked on the "Columbian Ode" for approximately
three years; and, when it was read by a chorus of five thousand
voices, she was justly proud that she had acted to honor poetry.
Although the ode was essentially an academic work, Miss Monroe

continued to reprint it in her future works because she felt that it marked a period of world optimism and expressed the spirit of the era. Of the exposition, she later wrote in her autobiography: "We seemed to discern a prophecy and a purpose in this gathering together of the nations. A new and wiser era was coming, when the marvelous discoveries of science would be used to promote the happiness and well-being of the race. My song of joy... did not sound extravagant."

Since the Columbian Exposition was an event of national importance, the details and news of its opening ceremonies were reported in the daily presses throughout the country. In its zealous interest to capture a lead on other newspapers, the *New York World* pre-empted the official opening of the fair and printed a purloined copy of the "Columbian Ode" before its public reading at the fair. When Miss Monroe's father brought suit against the *World*, he finally won a court decision in 1894 that awarded Harriet a settlement of five thousand dollars for damages. The *Monroe* case, important because it was without legal precedent, established the rights of authors to control their own unpublished works. Harriet had also received the unheard-of sum of one thousand dollars from the committee on ceremonies for the poem; this sum, coupled with her court settlement, was a sizable fortune to a poet who had struggled so long to perfect her art. There was, however, a long delay between the court decision and the final settlement.

The local notoriety of Miss Monroe's Columbian success did not transform her poetry, nor did it open any new avenues of acclaim or publication. The American public was still highly reserved in its acceptance of any poet, and the poetic taste of the times remained unimproved. Despite the unprecedented sum which she had received for the "Columbian Ode," Miss Monroe was never under the illusion that a poet could make his way in the world from the proceeds of his work. As a result, she earned her living in the world of literary journalism by writing countless articles on travels and art exhibitions.

Between the years 1891 and 1897, Miss Monroe published two books: the first, *Valeria and Other Poems,* was privately printed in 1891; the second, *John Wellborn Root,* appeared in 1897. Through the publication of her first volume of poetry, she achieved local success as a poet; and the appreciative recognition which the book received gave her status as an important local figure. When she offered to write the "Columbian Ode," she could point with some pride and justification to her previous publications as a claim for the task. *Valeria and Other Poems* is, by any critical standard, "a youthful work" with all of the inherent faults implied by that term. If the volume is no longer important as poetry, it still represents a signpost in Miss Monroe's struggle to find a style and a subject matter that would be acceptable as modern poetry.

Miss Monroe's second published work, *John Wellborn Root,* was a labor of love and a tribute to her brother-in-law. Mr. Root, married to Harriet's sister, Dora Louise, was a young architect of promise who possessed strong radical ideas. Under the persuasive influence of Mr. Root, Harriet achieved greater appreciation of American art and of the many directions which were open to the artist if he placed his faith in the possibilities around him. Like Ralph Waldo Emerson, Root preached the gospel that it was time to sever art from the courtly muses of Europe and to celebrate what was new and what was American in inspiration. Harriet's response to Mr. Root's brilliant personality was, of course, warm and human; and his artistic influence upon her was pervasive. Because of Root's untimely death just as the first fruits of his promising career were being realized, Miss Monroe felt the tragic irony of fate which destroys men so young and so full of potential greatness. Her touching memoir ponders this fickleness of life; and the book—in its quiet and restrained way—is an appreciation to Root for his artistic insight.

In 1897, when Miss Monroe finally received the *New York World*'s check for the settlement of her suit, she made hasty plans for a second European tour. Once again, Harriet was entertained by some of the most prominent literary figures of that day. While in London, she was introduced to and entertained by such notables as Alice Meynell, Francis Thompson, Thomas Hardy, Theodore Watts-Dutton, Fiona McLeod (William Sharp), Robert L. Stevenson, and Colonel Francis Higginson, the friend of Emily Dickinson and co-editor of her first published poems. Miss Monroe, unfortunately, did not leave a record of her impressions of literary London of the 1890's, except for a number of scattered remarks in her personal letters. Perhaps she was well aware of the *fin de siècle* attitudes in the air and their prophetic implications; and it is only by inference that we may guess the nature of her antipathy for the more exotic qualities of people like Aubrey Beardsley and Oscar Wilde. Certainly the philosophy of literature and art implicit in their lives and writing would have been against the grain of Harriet's more conservative attitudes. Nevertheless, she was conscious of the new drama of George Bernard Shaw and Henrik Ibsen and of the decadent cycle of poetry that was becoming fashionable in the hands of more traditional poets such as Rudyard Kipling and Lionel Johnson.

As she returned once more to her own country, what must have been her vision of the future of poetry in America? In Europe—and in England most particularly—she had witnessed tag ends of an effete poetry and a takeover by the traditionals who offered nothing new—men who were content to celebrate in anemic song the themes of fifty years past. Who on the American scene could change the tide? Was there a poet existing with a voice vigorous enough to be heard, a man to be taken seriously enough to be prophetic? Perhaps no such questions occurred to Miss Monroe; perhaps she was not ready to see herself moving toward a position of power in American poetry. But she was conscious of the void in American poetry—of the lack of an audience for poetry.

Miss Monroe had sojourned in Europe for a year, filling her days with new literary acquaintances and a round of visits to the famous art collections of the Continent. When she returned to her native city, she continued to earn a meager living from journalism. In 1898, she was successful in publishing several short poems in the *Atlantic* and in London's *Fortnightly Review*. Although she consistently submitted new poems to the various literary periodicals, the results were discouraging. Acceptances were rare; rebuffs were the more common reaction. One magazine, *Hampton's*, after specifically soliciting some verse from Harriet Monroe, rejected what she sent as unsuitable. "The verses we print," the editor wrote, "are rather of the progressive, uplift type, the kind that Kipling might do if he were writing in this country."[5] Throughout the decade of 1900-10, Miss Monroe tried diligently—often in the face of blank indifference— to find an outlet for serious poetry, for poems that were not merely echoes of staid thoughts and tired forms.

III   *The Drama Collection*

Miss Monroe's whole personality was drawn to the world
of art, and her interests in literary forms varied widely. From
her youngest days when her father had first introduced her to
the excitement of the theater, she had sought the magic formulas
for a successful play. In her heart of hearts, she was a poet,
but for a time the beauty and glamour of the stage caused her
to veer from her main objective. Her first effort in drama, *Valeria*,
was too derivative, too steeped in the noble heroics and bloody
tones of a Websterian revenge tragedy. Between the years 1895
and 1900 she wrote five plays, none of which was ever produced
professionally; but her collection of plays, *The Passing Show*,
was privately published in 1903. Perhaps the fact that most
encouraged her in the writing of these plays was the favorable
criticism given her work by people of reputation in the world
of drama. But the plays were essentially defective in the same
way that Henry James's dramatic efforts proved unsatisfactory.
Of one of Miss Monroe's first plays, *It Passes By*, William Archer
wrote: "No doubt on a second and more careful reading it would
become clearer to me, but I certainly received the impression
that it was too subtle and Browningesque for the stage."[6]

The Passing Show, clearly the best play of the collection, has
a scope and an architecture that show progression of theme,
one fortified by a number of symbolic elements that give richness
to the action. The human insight is penetrating, but there is
no real sharpness of character; they are, perhaps, too emblematic.
Occasionally, the dramatic verse dialogue lapses into Byronic
excess, with tones of great self-pity or empty emotion. Miss
Monroe was trying to weld together two elements: poetic drama
and modernity of subject. Generally, she chose real contemporary
situations involving human beings whose lives were not marked
by extraordinary character or adventure. In *The Passing Show*,
she succeeded to a greater degree than in any of her previous
attempts, but the technique and materials are not yet well suited.

The other plays of this collection are decidedly weak in
poetic language and in dramatic construction; but, as a literary
effort, the total collection displays an interesting direction for
her creative powers. In devoting her energies to poetic drama,
she was attempting to infuse a heightened and living power in

words and situations in a contemporary context. The remaining four plays of this group—*The Thunderstorm, At the Goal, After All,* and *A Modern Minuet*—are short works in which no attempt is made to move beyond a single scene. Moreover, the plays are peculiar for their artificial union of a kind of "grand poetic diction" with the imposition of mythological figures and symbols upon contemporary situations. Frequently, the dialogue of these minor verse dramas is incredibly dated and stilted: the verse seems more imposed than necessary, and the old traditions of elocution leap to mind as we read the plays. In a sense, Miss Monroe was herself a victim of the "poetic" excesses of a tradition that she later deplored as the editor of *Poetry.*

In fairness to Miss Monroe, we should note that she may have been keenly aware of these graceless elements. In part, she was responding to the temper of the times. Her plays were meant to please the taste of the era, and to criticize this kind of pilot effort by today's fashions puts an unfair burden on the works. Indeed, Miss Monroe, an avid theatergoer, had the expert criticism of the professionals in drama. They were very encouraging, and their advice was certainly not demanding a new direction in language or subject, despite the new drama of Henrik Ibsen and G. B. Shaw.

After her father's death in 1903, Miss Monroe continued her career as a journalist; and she resumed her position with the *Chicago Tribune* as art critic. She was, at this stage of her career, a highly informed and enthusiastic observer of the arts. During this same period, she also wrote feature articles for such quality magazines as *Atlantic* and the *Fortnightly Review.* We gain a sense of her diverse interests in pictorial art, sculpture, and architecture by the prolific nature of her journalistic efforts during this period. In her personal and professional papers deposited at the University of Chicago, there are many reviews and brief essays on the art world of Chicago of this era. Equally important to the abundance of her journalistic writing was the vibrancy and excitement for life and adventure that she put into those writings.

The unique aspect of Miss Monroe as a personality was her mental vigor—her determination not to be satisfied by slipping into a frame of mind that would allow life to pass unexamined. Nor did she ever allow her insecure income to prevent her

from taking an avid part in social life; her ever increasing circle
of friends soon embraced almost every person whose interest
in the arts was distinguished. Among her close confidants of
this period were such men as Albert Pinkham Ryder, the Amer-
ican painter, and Henry B. Fuller, the novelist and author of
the minor American classic, *The Cliff-Dwellers*. Fuller later
became a member of the first advisory committee for *Poetry*.

IV   *The New Century*

The years between 1900 and the founding of *Poetry* in 1912
were filled, therefore, with activities which advanced Miss
Monroe's prestige not only as a poet but as a person of adroit-
ness and social charm. Miss Gladys Campbell, one of the early
associates of *Poetry*, has described Miss Monroe as a rather
severe-looking little lady, as a woman of almost nondescript
appearance, but as a person whose intellectual charm made an
immediate impression. Her critical honesty, asserts Miss Camp-
bell, was always dependable. If Harriet was ever severe in her
critical comments about a writer, her severity was always tinged
with encouragement. No young poet was ever left feeling help-
less or hopeless.

The "middle years" of Miss Monroe's life were passing in
an unspectacular way. Her life was full, but the events which
later gave her a permanent place in American literary history
were unforeseen as she pursued a career which offered no great
challenge. The historical moment was long in developing; and,
as the first decade of the new century passed away, the con-
temporary poetry of the period seemed more and more without
a viable significance. If the literary scene seemed to be in a
state of slumber, other movements were developing to accentuate
the contrast; for the first decade of the new century had brought
immense progress to Chicago.

The changes made in the city since its disastrous fire in 1871
had produced an undreamed-of transformation not only in
commerce and industry but also in the arts. Chicago's strategic
position on Lake Michigan provided the site for the increasing
shipping industry; and the city was fast becoming the center
of the railroad network that fanned out to other cities in the
Midwest. Great fortunes were being made in the surge of

progress as Chicago was establishing itself as a great business center of the Midwest. The rising fortunes of Chicago and its civic leaders soon created a "high society," one acutely conscious of the city's cultural disadvantages. Any biographical sketch of Harriet Monroe is incomplete without a sense of the dynamism of her beloved Chicago.

The great name of the Potter Palmers and other equally distinguished families of Chicago gave glamor to the booming cultural scene. In architecture, the disappearance of the old baroque façades manifested a new spirit of freedom and experimentation. Many of the newly conceived buildings of the first decade are now charming—if ponderous—anachronisms that contrast to post-World War II innovations in architecture. Chicago is today rebuilding itself out of an old era of elegance —the era of Harriet Monroe. The great architectural feats of Louis Sullivan and Frank Lloyd Wright are landmarks of ingenuity for another age; and, just as this spirit of newness in architecture was changing the face of Chicago, the same spirit of aggressive experimentation and catholicity founded a renaissance in the world of the other arts.

The founding of the Chicago Art Institute and the birth of many theaters and music halls also testify to this vigorous interest. The entire range of the arts was improving during these early years, and Miss Monroe was part of this milieu. As an art critic, she was intimately acquainted with many artists and art dealers. Aware of the type of work which was being so handsomely rewarded by the Art Institute and other organizations, she felt a genuine sense of dejection about the fate of poetry. In spite of the generous feeling and receptivity accorded to drama, the other art forms—painting, music, poetry—were allowed to suffer almost total neglect.

It was not without some feelings of acrimony that Miss Monroe viewed the Art Institute's practice of giving large rewards to artists for their work while poetry was neither encouraged nor recognized. Why, she asked herself, was so much money being lavished on the plastic arts while poetry, perhaps the greatest of all arts, was being treated with indifference? To all her friends and business associates she repeated with challenging insistence: "Why was poetry left out of it—poetry, perhaps the finest of the fine arts, certainly the shyest and most elusive?—poetry which must have listeners, which cannot sing into a void?"[7] Her growing irritation later became the moving force from which a definite plan for *Poetry* emerged. The real plan for the magazine came much later, but it was preceded by a vague feeling of discontent with the status quo of the poet and by a decided irritation at the indifference with which poetry's self-styled supporters viewed the situation.

CHAPTER 2

The Founding of *Poetry*

I *The Poetic Scene: 1890-1912*

THE expansive period between the great Columbian Exposition and the international turmoil of World War I was one of national concentration on developing the great commercial and industrial potential of America. Amid this surge for material progress, poetry passed unnoticed and neglected. It could not be well integrated with the more demanding energies at work, nor could the country pause in its progress to wait for the art of poetry to emerge from its eclipse. The barrenness of American poetry at the turn of the century can be ascribed to many factors, and there were many honest reasons why the artist failed and was bound to fail. His inaction was dictated by the temper of the times; it could not be attributed merely to apathy or inattention on the part of the public.

Miss Monroe was impatient, ever anxious to make her personal concern for culture a more national and conscious concern. Contrary to her belief that the poet's voice had been silenced because of national apathy, the fact remains that there were simply no poets of stature working in those early years of the twentieth century. Even today, as we attempt to assess the poetic achievement of the first decade, the names which come to mind are those of slim and local talent, ones who are more nearly aligned with popular journalism or with a kind of commercial talent. The poetry of Emily Dickinson and Stephen Crane is exceptional. The latent talent of such poets as E. A. Robinson, Carl Sandburg, and Edgar Lee Masters came to its fullness much later. The impressive collection of names—poets of range and versatility—associated with the founding days of *Poetry* conjures a false notion of the poetic situation prior to 1912. The "Twilight Interval" between 1890 and 1912 was truly a moment of shadow from which no definite outline or direction of poetic talent could be predicted.

In an essay written many years earlier, and on a foreign soil, Matthew Arnold correctly analyzed the cultural status. In "The Modern Element of Literature," he defined the greatness of the Age of Pericles as the unique meeting of the man and the moment. The greatness of Grecian civilization might have passed into the bleak obscurity of history had not the poet emerged who correctly interpreted the meaning of his time and who preserved its magnificence and power for ages to come through his commanding revelation of meaning. The American cultural tradition required its interpreter, its poet of penetration and vision, to read the age aright, to give value and meaning to the multiplicity of facts. In great measure, Whitman had performed this heroic feat for nineteenth-century America. But, subsequently, no other poetic voice spoke with such clarity and penetration though the twentieth century waited with eager anticipation for its poet.

The poetic dilemma of the first decade of this century seemed to rest upon two widely divergent strains of song. In the reputed cultural centers of the East—New York and the great universities —the impress of poetry was still largely drawn from European sources. In America, there were no mature and gifted masters of poetic speech, no diction of native vitality and breadth. This absence of a modern direction can be seen in the poetry of such figures as E. C. Stedman, R. H. Stoddard, Eugene Field, and Richard Hovey. Indeed, in the case of Hovey, there is an almost literal devotion to contemporary British models and forms. With the possible exception of one or two poems, the work of these men rarely rises above acceptable journalistic verse.

The whole aura of the era was registered in Stedman's *An American Anthology* (1900): "*An American Anthology* was a work that gave historical perspective to its choices, and however generously Stedman represented the tastes and prejudices of his day which were schooled in an uncritical appreciation of Victorian verse, including the false vigor, mediocre diction, and belated Byronism of Bayard Taylor, his anthology brought to light submerged contrasts and vitalities in American poetry."[1] One significant point of *An American Anthology* is the pervasive display of an American talent which was dependent on another tradition for its inspiration, a dependency which was to rob the poetry of the period of a native vitality.

The second divergent strain in American poetry may be called regional, and it probably took its major impress from a Whitmanesque effort to portray real American life in poetry. Joaquin Miller, Edwin Markham, George Sterling, and James Whitcomb Riley were all contributors—each in different degrees—to a poetry which depended for its main effects on a regional and artificial poetic diction. Collectively, their poetry was an expression of stock emotional themes couched in a language of homely metaphor. A precursor of Edgar Lee Masters and Vachel Lindsay, James Whitcomb Riley had perhaps achieved the greatest public notoriety for this special brand of poetry. His work seemed to represent an American ideal that spoke directly to the heart of the people, to a great public majority which never concerned itself with subtleties or sophistication, to that audience which accepted poetry because it appealed to its inherent prejudices. The poetry of Riley and his followers relied heavily upon American dialect differences, and it offered relatively little that was new in subject matter. Its broad appeal seemed almost a barrier to further experimentation with form or subject matter.

If the American literary scene in 1900 was thus unripe for poetic innovation, the contemporary British poets were equally immersed in the more rigid patterns of the nineteenth century. Like their American counterparts, the British poets offered no guide to a new direction for English poetry. And, although the Georgian and Edwardian poetry still constitutes a more formidable body of permanently interesting work than does a comparable body of poetry produced in America during the same period, neither the British nor the American poets were generating any new approaches to their art. Where it was not frankly regional—as in the work of Riley—American poetry was, in summary, more apt to be a reflection of British traditional poetry. The obscurity to which the American and British minor poets of this epoch have been relegated is itself an indication of even their failure to be a testament of their reliance upon the traditionalism of another age.

If England could boast of such poets as Rudyard Kipling and

Thomas Hardy, its minor poets—Alfred Noyes, Laurence Binyon, William Watson, James Flecker, and others—today share an equal status of obscurity with their American counterparts—George Sterling, Bayard Taylor, and Joaquin Miller. Kipling, Hardy, and the more consciously classical Robert Bridges were pursuing a type of poetry that must be labeled "traditional." With the possible exception of Hardy, many of these traditional poets shared a popularity equal to that of Longfellow and James Whitcomb Riley. The poetry that was being produced in England and America at the turn of the century was not addressing itself to the new age: "Unrest of soul and introspection had little place, whether the poet was young or old. Poets sang and told stories as if that were the purpose of poetry. There was high seriousness, but it often went with high spirits."[2] In varying degrees, the restrained poetry of these men sought to continue and renew the tradition of English poetry; and a great part of the nation was still loyal to its old tastes. The need to break with the "old tastes" was increasingly apparent among the younger and less well-established poets of both nations. However, the almost inevitable fate of any new poetry which deviated from the established tone and form of the prevailing poetic expectation was neglect and rejection.

II A New Publishing Venture

For the poet, the great difficulty of achieving publication and the general failure of public notice were simply accepted facts in the publishing world. Poetry was not a rewarding business venture; and, unless a publisher could be assured of a modest return on his investment, his reluctance toward poetry was understandable—if regrettable. Few publishers were in a position to gamble with profits. What they consented to publish had to be at least marked by some signs of familiarity, some omens of success. Frequently, the established poet found a ready audience; but the new poet suffered an enforced silence.

If book publication was nearly impossible, the placement of single poems was equally difficult—unless the poem conformed to some pre-established notions. Even the main literary magazines of the times were reluctant to feature poetry; thus, poetry was invariably overshadowed by a more topical and ponderous prose. The future of poetry—if it were to have a future—had to be molded by the advanced guard, by the poets and by those whom they could enlist who were convinced that poetry was not merely a decorative appendage to culture, but necessary and integral for a developed, articulate culture.

The problems of publishing were only one of the many difficulties which faced the serious modern poet in the early decades. More significant were the literary attitudes shared by many people in positions of importance. Frequently, these attitudes expanded beyond poetry and reflected national and political biases. The whole relationship of Realism in literature was affected because of its obvious implications of the worth and merit of unheroic experience. Though to re-create the whole aura of the "genteel" tradition which basically controlled the tone of literature in this period would require an argument of great detail, the most salient features of this conflict can be seen in the elite situation which dominated the artistic and literary world of Chicago in 1910.

In the middle 1890's, Chicago could be justly proud of its promotion of the arts; it possessed one of the finest auditoriums for the performing arts in the Midwest, a place which became a mecca for those interested in the cultural life of the city. Around this nebulous group of citizens there emerged an informal club, The Little Room, which met each Friday afternoon after the symphony concert. "The Little Room was neither exclusively intellectual nor exclusively artistic; its importance lay not in its production of art, but in the degree to which it both comprised and symbolized the largest official acceptance of the arts as a living cultural force which Chicago had been able to achieve."[3]

The members of The Little Room were drawn from among Chicago's most leisured and cultivated social level. The group was the center of meeting for a wealthy, patronizing class whose activity in the art world gave substance to a cultural veneer they sought to spread over the more unpleasant aspects of Chicago as a frontier town. The roster of members—formal and informal—included a large number of people intent upon instilling the "genteel" influence into the literary culture of Chicago. To this end, a number of literary organs devoted themselves: "From 1885 until about 1905, there was a stream of periodicals and publishers through which the genteel tradition maintained itself in print and attempted to establish itself in fact as the dominant cultural element in Chicago."[4]

Such literary periodicals as Hobart Chatfield-Taylor's *America* or the more ephemeral *Literary Life* had a large local appeal, partially because the editorial opinion reflected a striving for the best in literature and art. The tone of these periodicals conveyed an almost missionary zeal as the editors sought to raise the taste of the public. Frequently, the editors extended the limits of literary criticism to voice political and social opinion; for they regarded literature as one instrument in molding an aristocratic culture. Because of the cultural and social changes of the last fifty years, many of the social positions which the editors of the magazines held now seem faintly silly; nevertheless, their voices remained for its time cogent and commanding ones for the upward movement in literature. There was much of the old Arnoldian desire to create a "culture of perfection" in their efforts, but they lacked a broad sense of sympathy with the realities of society as it existed at the time. Without a real awareness of their place in the historical pattern, these men were fighting against the vulgarism of their day, and they reflected all of the less attractive elements of the "genteel" tradition.

Inevitably, Harriet Monroe was the product of this cultural milieu. Unhampered by any strong political or social motives, she nevertheless viewed literature as contributory to cultural betterment. Although without personal wealth, Harriet Monroe was an intimate of The Little Room and with its more wealthy arbiters of social taste; and she shared many of their assumptions about the nature and function of literature. The later radicalism of *Poetry* frequently obscures Miss Monroe's place in the "genteel protest" because it tends to impute a kind of foresight and catholicity which she did not possess—although she was certainly to adopt and modify her views as the age progressed.

Miss Monroe's associations with the controlling literary elect of Chicago had an obvious significance upon her own poetic productions. Her work of this period was a general reflection of the "genteel" tradition, and the insularity of the local literati restricted her vision. Desperately pursuing a career on the fringes of literature, she took every opportunity to present her poems before the public; but editorial disregard was the usual response. Such journals as existed were not eager to print poetry; and, if they did, the editors demanded a close echo of James Whitcomb Riley's "unabashed sentimentality." The plight of the rejected poet was not merely the fate of Miss Monroe but also that of her literary friends. In spite of many defeats, Harriet Monroe had been faithful to her craft; she had persevered over the long years.

In the few years preceding the actual founding of *Poetry* in 1911, she must have occasionally viewed her career as poet with feelings of futility. She had had her successes, but they must have appeared as high points in a career otherwise undistinguished and without sustained recognition. But ever resourceful, Miss Monroe was not easily deterred, and she had given too much of herself to poetry. With a kind of spinsterish pluck, she decided that, even if no one else cared for serious poetry, she did. And it might be her mission to do something about it. Miss Monroe, now fifty years of age, had reached a point in life when most people would feel that the days of adventure and accomplishment were behind them. But Miss Monroe always looked forward; and, when most people would have thought that the time for action was over, she began a new stage in life, a stage that was to be her most significant contribution to the shape of modern poetry.

With the advice of her friend Chatfield-Taylor, she devised a plan to create a magazine exclusively for poets, a place where the young poet could appeal to an audience denied him by the conventional journals of the day. If her efforts were not to be abortive, she knew that she must plan well and carefully; thus, for two years, amid her other activities, she carried on her campaign to bring *Poetry* into existence. During these two years of preparation, Miss Monroe continued to write free-lance feature articles for Hearst's *Evening Post*; she was at the same time art critic for the *Chicago Tribune*, a position that gave her a series of interesting contacts and friendships in the art world. These years were a time of revolutionary change in the arts of painting and sculpture, and the aggressive spirit of the plastic arts had been rewarded by popular recognition and audience attention. There were no similar rewards for the poet.

In devising her plans for *Poetry*, Miss Monroe attacked the problem of finances first. If the magazine could not be assured a reasonable life span, the venture might not be worth pursuing. From the very beginning, she had certain preconceptions of the nature of the magazine: it must be financially sound and independent from outside pressure on editorial policy; it must strive to display the best poetry being written at the time; it must be a force of influence for new creative effort. Her long experience in journalism and her acquaintanceship with the little magazines such as *America* and the *Dial* had convinced her that the subtlety of financial pressure inevitably controlled editorial content. To gain the independence which she demanded as the first requisite, Miss Monroe controlled all the stages of the funding of the magazine. Her many contacts in the literary and art world gave her a special entree to many of the financially influential people of Chicago.

Miss Monroe planned her strategy with great calculation, for she knew that no businessman would contribute to the airy cause of an elusive and unpopular art unless she could argue a sound case in its favor. The one great element that worked in her favor was the chauvinistic pride of Chicagoans in their city, and she was able to appeal to this sense of pride. Chicago's industrial and financial dominance in the Midwest had long been established, but there was always a painful consciousness that the city was second-rate in the field of the arts. Although great strides had been made in architecture, music, and painting, the literary efforts of the city were without vitality or influence. Miss Monroe was offering the businessmen—and, therefore, the city itself—the opportunity to redress this failure in the local cultural scene. One of her strongest arguments for *Poetry*, it succeeded very well.

It was her hope that she would be able to secure sufficient funds for her magazine to continue publication for at least five years. To achieve this objective, it would be necessary to secure a minimum of five thousand dollars annually for the five-year period. In current times, five thousand dollars may seem an extraordinarily small sum, but in 1910 it represented a significant investment—at least from the vantage point of the frugal maiden lady. If Miss Monroe could secure pledges of one hundred dollars a year for five years from fifty contributors, the magazine would be realizable and independent. To Miss Monroe, the goal seemed awesome; but, to her great surprise, the project was met with genuine enthusiasm, and money was quickly pledged.

It would be ungracious to pass over this stage of the magazine's development without further comment and praise for the initial group of contributors who made *Poetry* possible. Special recognition must be given to Chatfield-Taylor. In her autobiography, Miss Monroe has recorded her debt to him for the inciting notion of a "magazine for poets" and for the general plan of securing financial resources. She wrote: "My confidence gradually gained headway, and a talk with my Little Room friend Hobart C. Chatfield-Taylor—novelist, lover of the arts, man of culture, wealth, and social prominence—gave shape and purpose to it, and brought forth a definite plan."[5]

The major work of campaigning for funds occupied most of Miss Monroe's spare time from September, 1911, to June, 1912. As the project gained momentum, she received support in the leading local newspapers. When she invaded the office of a foremost executive, he was generally aware of her mission and succumbed to her appeal. At times, she met with disinterest or amusement for her efforts; but, while some may have thought the scheme foolish and destined to fail, she never became disheartened nor allowed her enthusiasm to waver. After six long months of constant campaigning, she exceeded her goal. Her list of first subscribers was a brave band of Chicagoans who had faith in Miss Monroe's determination to do the job. "To say that Miss Monroe's first list of guarantors read like a social register would only tell half the story; the truth was that many of these patrons of the arts were artists themselves and only incidentally members of the first families."[6] The hope of capturing all the support of the wealthy citizens was not fully realized, but the backers she did get proved the better because their interest was at once personal and altruistic.

Once assured of sound financial backing for the magazine, Miss Monroe turned her attention to the second major task of her project—to enlist new poets of talent and promise. She now had something unique to offer the poets—a place to display their works and to be paid for their poems. In her search for new poets, Miss Monroe seems never to have doubted her critical

powers and her competence to spot new talent, and her first
step in surveying the current poetic situation was to read as
widely as possible among the newly published works of poetry.
As often as her other journalistic activities permitted, she visited
the Chicago Public Library to read the journals and books of
poetry. She was, of course, well aware of the lower status ac-
corded to poetry by the leading periodicals of the day, and
she knew that much of what she was reading was frequently
an unfair sampling of any poet's work. She was able to cast
aside a good deal of verse that was merely "verse"—the kind
of poem that ran true to the conventional form and to the
subject matter imposed upon it by editors unconcerned with
poetry as an art.

During her reading, she compiled a comprehensive list of
poets. From this more inclusive list, she later narrowed down
a more selected group of poets who "interested" her. She based
the choice on their past achievements and, in the case of young
poets, on the indication of promise which they displayed. Having
compiled the selected list, Miss Monroe pondered the ways in
which she could best gain the writers' enthusiasm and find the
necessary audience for them. In Miss Monroe's mind, she was
caught between the cross fire of two opposing, but lethargic,
armies. On the one hand, the general public was indifferent
to the state of poetry; and on the other hand, the poets them-
selves were failing to live up to the dynamism of the times:
"Innovations were sporadic, and contrary to the general prac-
tice and prejudice of the time."[7] Many of the established poets
were writing "the same old thing in the same old academic way."

The awesome attitude and the Miltonic austerity of much
of the contemporary poetry irritated Miss Monroe; for she
sought a new poetry that expressed a more sympathetic humanity,
that was drawn from the modern life of man, and that had
relevance to the present time. Thus, her selected list of poets
had certain elements in common: they were engaged in making
poetry a living vehicle for new ideas, and they were unabashed
experimenters in poetic form. If *Poetry* was to produce its
desired effect, it would have to assault not this public but poetic
indifference to change: "It was this indifference that I started
out to combat, this dry conservatism that I wished to refresh
with living waters from a new spring. Here and there were hints

of freshness.... Could I find and follow these traces of a new
vitality in the art? There must be poets—could I search them
out and assemble them, and find the necessary public for them?"[8]
In August and early September, 1912, Miss Monroe sent a
"poet's circular" to each of her "selected" poets. In addition
to being an "invitation," this circular had a distinctive value
because it set forth the initial ideals and objectives of the
magazine. After explaining the financial basis on which the new
magazine was founded, the circular continued as follows:

The success of this first American effort to encourage the pro-
duction and appreciation of poetry, as the other arts are encouraged,
by endowment, now depends on the poets. We offer them:
First, a chance to be heard in their own place, without the limita-
tions imposed by the popular magazine. In other words, while the
ordinary magazines must minister to a large public little interested
in poetry, this magazine will appeal to, and it may be hoped will
develop, a public primarily interested in poetry as an art, as the
highest, most complete human expression of truth and beauty.
Second, within space limitations imposed at present by the small
size of our monthly sheaf—from sixteen to twenty-four pages the
size of this—we hope to print poems of greater length and of more
intimate and serious character than the other magazines can afford
to use. All kinds of verse will be considered—narrative, dramatic,
lyric—quality alone being the test of acceptance. Certain numbers
may be devoted entirely to a single poem, or a group of poems by
one person; except for a few editorial pages of comment and review.
Third, besides the prize above mentioned, we shall pay con-
tributors. The rate will depend on the subscription list, and will
increase as the receipts increase, for this magazine is not intended
as a money-maker but as a public-spirited effort to gather together
and enlarge the poet's public and to increase his earnings. If we
can raise the rate paid for verse until it equals that paid for paintings,
etchings, statuary, representing as much ability, time and reputation,
we shall feel that we have done something to make it possible for
poets to practice their art and be heard. In addition, we should like
to secure as many prizes, and as large, as are offered to painters and
sculptors at the annual exhibitions in our various cities.
In order that this effort may be recognized as just and necessary,
and may develop for this art a responsive public, we ask the poets
to send us their very best verse. We promise to refuse nothing
because it is too good, whatever be the nature of its excellence.
We shall read with special interest poems of modern significance,

but the most classic subject will not be declined if it reaches a
high standard of quality.

In addition to the printed circular, Miss Monroe frequently
included a personal letter in which she referred individually
to a poet's work and expressed her desire that he would make
an early contribution of some of his verses. Within a few weeks
after sending the letters, enthusiastic replies arrived. Miss Monroe
then knew that her plan was to be successful.

Among the many encouraging responses, the most enthusiastic
one came from Ezra Pound in England. He expressed his disgust
at the present state of American poetry, analyzed the causes
and the effects it was producing in the minds of serious poets,
reproached the degeneracy of American academic institutions,
and otherwise voiced his general contempt for the intellectual
milieu in America—but he offered Miss Monroe every assistance
in her plan to restore poetry to its proper dignity. In response
to Miss Monroe's request for contributions of poetry, Pound
wrote: "Can you teach the American poet that poetry *is* an art,
an art with a technique, with media, an art that must be in
constant flux, a constant change of manner, if it is to live?"[9]

Pound evidently believed that *Poetry* could accomplish this
high goal, for he offered his services as foreign correspondent,
and Miss Monroe eagerly accepted his help. Indeed, this alliance
gave the magazine much of its excitement in the early years,
for Pound had access to many new poets in England and on
the Continent. In turn, he was eager to place many new poets
before the public, and *Poetry* was an opportunity for him to
wield a good deal of influence in the literary life of London
and Paris. The benefit was mutual, although Pound's demanding
temperament later caused him to resign his post as foreign
correspondent.

The first band of editors, with Harriet Monroe as the senior
member, included Edith Wyatt and Alice Corbin Henderson,
the wife of an artist in Lake Bluff and a long-time friend of
the Monroe family. Although circumstances made it impossible
for Edith Wyatt to assist fully in the duties of editorship, she
was active as a member of a three-man Advisory Committee,
along with Henry B. Fuller and Hobart Chatfield-Taylor. Ac-
quainted from their old association with The Little Room group,

Edith Wyatt was a special friend of Miss Monroe. A poet and a novelist, Miss Wyatt had a keen, Bryn-Mawr trained mind that was quick to recognize excellence in poetry. Their common concern for the fate of the poet and poetry made Miss Monroe and Miss Wyatt energetic and sympathetic critics. The extent of their mutual sympathy is especially evident in the similarity of the poetic subject matter of each. Edith Wyatt's *The Wind in the Corn* (1917) expressed many of the themes dear to Harriet's own poetry—the high energy and color of the western regions of America and the spirit of joyousness and beauty in life itself.

Alice Corbin Henderson, the first associate editor, strongly influenced the shape of the magazine during her short tenure. "Without her influence Miss Monroe's paper might have been ... narrower in its scope and less epoch-making in its effect.... The influence she had on the early course of *Poetry* was decisive."[10] In the Harriet Monroe collection at the University of Chicago, Mrs. Henderson's letters reveal a forceful and outspoken personality, and she frequently delivered short and pointed criticism at such figures as Amy Lowell and Ezra Pound. She may well have been responsible for tempering Harriet Monroe's attitudes toward Lowell and Pound from one of reserve and hesitation to a more tolerant, indeed enthusiastic, appreciation for the special talent of these innovative poets. If Harriet Monroe and Edith Wyatt's earlier commitment was to "genteel" literature, Mrs. Henderson was more attuned to new trends in poetry. "Much of the attitude of the magazine towards experimentation in new techniques which was then beginning is due to her. She was more susceptible even than Harriet herself to the possibilities of the future."[11]

With her editorial staff assembled, Miss Monroe found quarters for her "little magazine" in the front room of a remodeled mansion on Chicago's famous Near North Side. With some borowed furniture, a few old rugs, and a poet's chair for visiting poets, she was ready to bring forth the first issue of her magazine which she had determined to call *Poetry: A Magazine of Verse*. Exactly when and why she selected the subtitle is never explained in any of her writings. If it was true that she realized that everything to be printed would not be poetry but merely verse, then the subtitle represents still another example of her carefulness in allowing for a margin of error in human judgment.

Miss Monroe had also chosen a motto from Whitman for her magazine: "To have great poets, a nation must have a great audience." The motto exactly suited the purposes of *Poetry* as she envisioned them at this initial stage. Although Whitman's notion of the need for "a great audience" was later severely criticized by Pound, Miss Monroe knew well in advance that the educative process and the influence that her magazine would have must be dependent upon a broad base of acceptance and sympathy: it could not assume the editorial policy of delivering great poetry from on high to a skeptical and unwilling audience. The whole process was to be a dynamic one, with both the poet and the audience engaged in a new appreciative effort.

The history of the founding of *Poetry* is, of course, a minor movement in the larger record of modern poetry; and the details of this account recall a number of names and events that have slipped to the subsurface of that larger record, but the contribution made by each of these early associates has its own significance. Miss Monroe was indeed fortunate in the generosity of people who contributed financial security and intellectual energy during the initial stages of *Poetry*. Without this subtle combination of enthusiasm and determination, *Poetry* might have been a less forceful vehicle for poetic innovation and renewal. However, the independent courage of its first editor was permanently stamped on the magazine.

CHAPTER 3

Poetry: *A Magazine of Verse*

I *The Original Contract—The First Year*

THE publication of the first issue of *Poetry* in 1912 is viewed by many literary historians as a point of demarcation in American Poetry—as an event in our history which was decisive in releasing new energies in American poetic creativity. The time of publication was fortuitous, and the latent literary talent of the Midwest emerged in an unsuspected renascence of achievement that has since become a part of the permanent literature of America. Bernard Duffey has declared that *"Poetry* was for a crucial time the nexus of all twentieth-century poetic life, and, in admitting the Chicago poets to that life, it brought them full into the twentieth-century world."[1] One of Miss Monroe's ideals for *Poetry* was that it would be a force, a stimulus, for new directions in poetry. Today, the year 1912 clearly marks the significance of those "new directions" for modern American poetry.

In the years 1911 and 1912, Harriet Monroe's energies were absorbed in the process of securing a financial base for her magazine and in inviting the interest of a great many poets for the new periodical. She was very successful in both endeavors. But despite the carefulness of two years of planning, the first issue of *Poetry* encountered an unexpected difficulty. In the final month of preparation for publication, Miss Monroe received notice that a rival magazine bearing an almost identical title was being organized in Boston by William Stanley Braithwaite. Realizing that Boston would have the advantage over Chicago in any literary enterprise and trying to protect the right of precedence to her title, Miss Monroe determined to publish an early issue, thereby successfully gaining the initiative over her eastern rivals. Years later, after the Boston poetry journal had failed, Braithwaite became one of *Poetry's* more denigrating critics; he constantly proclaimed that Miss Monroe's magazine was declining in power and importance. But Miss Monroe had saved the right to her title by publishing her first issue of *Poetry* in October, 1912.

The initial issue contained a number of short lyric works by Ezra Pound, Emilia Stuart Lorimer, Helen Dudley, Arthur Ficke, and Grace Hazard Conkling. Because Miss Monroe was forced to move ahead of schedule, she managed to complete the issue by including William Vaughn Moody's posthumous work, "I am the Woman." Few could argue about the competency of the poems printed; and, if they lacked innovative fire, the haste of preparing the first issue helps explain the dilemma.

The new magazine was amply reported in the national press, and generous praise was given to the adventure. Frequently, the newspapers' commentary was gently satiric. To the eastern news columnists, the appearance of *Poetry* was interpreted as Chicago's unceasing bid for cultural recognition, a bid that ran counter to the all too firmly established image of Chicago as a "frontier town," a center for industry and meat-packing operations. If the efforts of *Poetry* were accepted as less than genuine, Miss Monroe had the consolation of knowing she could refute the lie. Within weeks after the first copy had appeared, the *Poetry* offices were being inundated with poems and letters of congratulations from all over the world.

Although Miss Monroe had launched her magazine with great care to detail, she could not have been expected to foresee all the possibilities before her. In the first editorial, entitled "The Motive of the Magazine," she set forth a rationale for *Poetry*. The article repeats many of the arguments that were so persuasive in capturing financial support for the magazine. In spite of the general failure of the "quality" magazines to print good poetry, Miss Monroe insisted—with a kind of intuitive certainty— that good poetry existed. It was, she declared, the aim of *Poetry* to encourage and print the best poetry available. The commercial publishers were traditionally the rear guard because their editors would accept a writer only after the advanced guard had proved that he was, or could be made, commercially profitable.[2] *Poetry* was independent of the profit motive; therefore, it was free to accept all poetry of excellence as literature. "The test, limited by ever-fallible human judgment, is to be quality alone."[3] The remaining months of 1912 were exciting ones for *Poetry*. Harriet Monroe and her associate editors were quick to realize that the magazine had released new forces and that the young poets were responding eagerly to the opportunity to have their works displayed. The daily mail in *Poetry*'s office expanded beyond expectation, and the magazine achieved a rapport with many new poets. Pound's poem, "To Whistler—American," which appeared in the first issue of the magazine, had set the tone for the challenge. His reference to middle-class Americans as a "mass of dolts" had irritated many readers, but Miss Monroe interpreted the phrase as "the first hint of new forces at work in art." Hopefully, she felt that a whole generation of Victorian-American mildness was being left behind and that the new poet would be free to speak his honest conviction in a more energized voice.

In the few years of Pound's association with *Poetry*, Pound gave the magazine much of its glamour—and most of its controversial tone. In the second issue, he was responsible for procuring some poems from the new English poet, Richard Aldington, whom Pound described in the Notes (*Poetry*, I [March, 1913]) as "one of the Imagistes, a group of ardent Hellenists who are pursuing interesting experiments in *vers libre*; trying to attain in English certain subtleties of cadence of the kind which Mallarmé and his followers have studied in French." The full impact of the Imagist movement was to come months later, but *Poetry* had the satisfaction of being in the forefront and of recognizing the significant trends of change.

The editorial in the second issue emphasized Harriet Monroe's concept that *Poetry* would not take a restrictive attitude toward what she called "minor poetry." "Fear has been expressed," she wrote, "by a number of friendly critics that *Poetry* may become a house of refuge for minor poets." Since no contemporary could utter the final verdict, *Poetry* and its editors welcomed poetry from all quarters; and, however minor the poetry might have seemed at a given time, it could eventually take its place in the larger pattern of a single poet's work, or it might remain as a singularly excellent effort, respected for its "tenacity of life"—a little masterpiece, not a great one. To fortify this inclusive policy, Miss Monroe declared that *Poetry* must remain "free of entangling alliances with any single class or school," a point of policy that saved the magazine from extreme enthusiasm for any one cause or trend. The wisdom of Miss Monroe's "open-door" policy has proved its worth in countless cases, and today the magazine continues to rely heavily on the same principles.

With the publication of the third issue, *Poetry* struck an unqualified tone of literary success. The little volume included five new poems by William Butler Yeats, Rabindranath Tagore's translation of the six "Gitanjali," and poems by John Reed, Alice Meynell, George Sterling, and Alice Corbin. It was clear that the magazine had an international scope. In all, it was a brilliant issue for a magazine only three months old. Few poets could now deny the prestige of appearing in *Poetry*; and, while its reputation for excellence continued to grow, so did the volume of contributions. The December issue was able to close the year with the firm assurance that *Poetry* was a provocative and established magazine.

The year 1913 was an even more decisive one for Miss Monroe. She had begun her editorial tasks with certain ingrained preferences for American poetry and with the firm conviction that the creative effort was a dynamic venture. At times, her chauvinism led her to print works that were of questionable quality. On other unfortunate occasions, she accepted unseen works from minor poets of reputation, only to discover that the poems were disappointing. These few errors, however, were confined to the earliest days of the magazine when it was doubtful if there would be sufficient good poems to fill an issue.

Although Miss Monroe herself wrote little narrative poetry, she was so fond of the form that she had to be firmly persuaded by her associate editors not to select a narrative instead of a dramatic or lyric poem. Moreover, despite her critical insight into the works of other poets, she had little self-criticism regarding her own poetry. Throughout her career as editor, she printed many of her own poems in *Poetry* that did not equal the standards of other contributors. But these were the limitations of almost any editor, or almost any poet, in the sensitive position of being an interim judge of greatness.

In theory, Miss Monroe was convinced that poetry must draw its sustenance from the current of life in the present. If *Poetry* favored the more experimental verse forms over traditional metrics, the reason was not a rejection of the past but a stronger desire to turn to the new expanding possibilities of language. She opened the New Year of 1913 with one of her best discoveries: Vachel Lindsay's "General William Booth Enters into Heaven." Lindsay's poem exactly fitted Miss Monroe's sense of the daring attempt to make poetry do more than it had been capable of before 1912. One critic found the poem "daring and shocking and upsetting" but deeply reverent. The relatively recent printing of a James Dickey poem, "May Day Sermon," in the *Atlantic Monthly* (April, 1967), has caused a similar reaction; but the courage of the editors inevitably rests upon the pioneer effort of a woman like Harriet Monroe who was willing to challenge the prevailing tastes and expectations of her audience. Indeed, the substantial fame that came to Lindsay in later years owes much to Miss Monroe's encouragement at a crucial stage in his career.

Besides initiating an audience to the unconventional and sonorous rhythms of Lindsay, the same issue of *Poetry* contained several "reflections and translations" by "H. D., Imagiste." Pound, who was diligently at work in London fostering the Imagist doctrine, was clearly under the aegis of T. E. Hulme and his demands for a clean, hard, dry verse. Hulme's classical theory coalesced almost completely with Pound's own preconceptions of poetical concentration on the sacredness of language as poetic vehicle. In championing the early works of Richard Aldington and "H. D.," Pound saw himself at the center of a new movement, and he convinced Miss Monroe for a time that Imagism was the only significant and most likely permanent trend in new poetry. Pound's own "expansive pride as the founder of a new school of poetry"[4] was to lead Miss Monroe herself and *Poetry* into a series of personal and public controversies. But, for the time, *Poetry* at least was printing works that were provocative.

Throughout 1913, *Poetry* was deeply immersed in the Imagist movement; and Harriet Monroe was initially eager to accept many of the contributions which Pound secured from young British poets. Miss Monroe was attracted to the Imagist sense for precise technique and language and for the free-verse form—two elements that coincided with her concept of poetic modernity. The fact that the formulation of the Imagist doctrine was still in the developing stage also had great appeal because of the timeliness and dynamic elements of the process. Imagism seemed to be a poetry in action that was growing out of a clash of views. In Miss Monroe's mind, it was live poetry, not a by-product of the academies, in which poets were grappling with the demands of art with the concentration and seriousness that art demanded.

In March, 1913, *Poetry* printed two documents that were central to the new movement: F. S. Flint's "History of Imagism" and Pound's "A Few Don't's by an Imagiste." The Imagist poems had impressed a number of *Poetry*'s critics as slight performances, and the two articles were intended both as rationale and as a programmatic method for new aspiring poets. Pound's imperative list of negatives was an unabashed echo of T. E. Hulme's endorsement of a hard and dry poetry. Even Hulme's characterization of Romantic poetry as damp and limp appeared by implication in Pound's "don'ts" for the poet. Today, the theoretic issues and implications of Imagism have been more fully explored and related to the psychology of larger literary issues, and the fundamental question of the use of poetry has been altered in light of the Imagist movement. The insistent demand for a sharply focused and precisely delineated image has become the hallmark of modern poetry. A special devotion to words as the medium of organized emotion defines the Imagists, and their refusal to enter into the largely discursive or narrative forms of poetry suggests how carefully they held to the dogma of precision.

For the Imagists' own times, the issues and ramifications were, of course, more revolutionary. With Imagism, the rise of New Criticism took shape; and the expanded definition of the novel form—under the hands of James Joyce and Virginia Woolf—may well owe a debt to the Imagist insistence on precision and on the presentation of "an intellectual and emotional complex in an instant of time." The immediacy and simultaneity of the poetry—along with its almost epigrammatic sparseness—demanded a totally new orientation on the part of the reader; and both Pound and Flint tried to provide a theory for the new poetry in the first magazine to give effective promotion to the Imagists.

Throughout 1913 many new poets were being printed, and *Poetry* had the honor to introduce such midwestern poets as Carl Sandburg, Edgar Lee Masters, and, as noted, Vachel Lindsay. In substance, Pound disagreed with the printing of many of these poets; and, if he was not actually hostile, he was at least unenthusiastic because he felt that the space might be better devoted to Imagistic experiment. To print such poets as Sandburg and Lindsay was, however, a point of particular editorial pride for Harriet Monroe because the emergence of such midwestern poets confirmed her belief that what was required for good poetry to flourish was opportunity. She and Pound simply did not share the same attitude toward American literature; and, to his supposedly more sophisticated vantage point, Miss Monroe was timid and provincial. The one poet to emerge who pleased both the editor and her errant foreign correspondent was Amy Lowell.

Miss Lowell had responded with enthusiasm to Harriet Monroe's "poet's circular." The editor, who had spotted Lowell's work in earlier publications, thought it possessed finish and quality; thus, when Miss Lowell submitted several poems and an encouraging financial contribution, Harriet was delighted to consider her work. The future relationship between these two highly charged personalities was marked by professional respect, but they differed too widely as individuals ever to create a warm friendship.

Miss Lowell was the product of wealth and culture; her famous name was a mark of intellectual respect and breeding, and she always lived up to this public image. Given her background and personality, she simply could not brook criticism, no matter how slight. This reaction was especially true about her poetry. There is no question that Amy Lowell was an exacting and rigorous poet, and she was always sensitive to any implication of error in detail. As an editor, however, Miss Monroe frequently offered alternative suggestions of words or lines to her contributing poets, and she rarely met with an adamant defense. Miss Lowell, exceedingly defensive about such

suggestions, usually countered any requests with a verbose and
stuffy rationale, frequently citing authorities for certain gram-
matical points or other details. And, if any changes were in-
advertently made, she was furious.

On one occasion, when *Poetry* printed a Lowell poem, one
line was dropped because of a printing error. Unfortunately,
this omission changed the tone and content, giving the poem
an implied sexual meaning. By the time Miss Lowell became
aware of the error, the magazine had already been distributed
to its many subscribers; she nevertheless demanded that all
extant copies of *Poetry* be recalled and destroyed. She was no
doubt rightfully irritated by this unfortunate mishap since
she genuinely believed that her reputation as a poet was at
stake. For her part, Miss Monroe regretted the error; and the
two women finally worked out a compromise solution for cor-
recting the manuscript in the next issue. The unfortunate event
did little, however, to foster rapport between the editor and
Miss Lowell.

It would be an error to suggest that these two women failed
to appreciate each other's excellent qualities. There were mis-
understandings and differences of opinion, but the folders of
Amy Lowell's letters in the Harriet Monroe Collection display
a long-standing concern and interest in the activities of *Poetry*.
If Amy Lowell could be pompous, she could also be a serious,
concerned artist willing to expend much energy and effort to
foster the ends of *Poetry*. And, despite the differences of approach
and temperament, Harriet Monroe and Amy Lowell carried on
a guarded relationship to the apparent benefit of each.

In September, 1913, when Miss Lowell sailed for Europe,
she carried a letter of introduction from Harriet Monroe to
Ezra Pound. By this time, Miss Lowell herself was very much
imbued with the Imagist doctrine; and she identified her poetic
efforts with much of the work that Pound and his associates
were doing in London. Again, two strong personalities were
to meet and breed inevitable conflicts. Pound was, of course,
ever ready to give imperative advice; and Lowell was prepared
to resist being drawn into the group. To account for the activities
of these two poets, as they shifted for leadership in the London
literary life, is not germane to the history of *Poetry*, except to
point out that Pound himself soon lost interest in the Imagist

cause and shifted his allegiance to the Vorticist movement.
Before defecting, however, Pound, aided by Amy Lowell, pub-
lished an anthology, *Les Imagistes,* containing much of the
work of the "newer school" and patterned on the previously
successful *Georgian Anthology* by Edward March. "Almost im-
mediately after the publication of *Les Imagistes* in 1914, Pound's
interest in the Imagist poets began to waver and he turned
his energy to another movement, this time not in poetry but in
painting."[5] Miss Lowell did not follow Pound's lead, but returned
to her native Boston and tried to revive and sustain the interest
that Imagism had aroused in America.

In the midst of all this contention for leadership, *Poetry* con-
tinued to print the works of the Imagists; but, with characteristic
restraint, Miss Monroe regarded the movement as one direction,
as one strain of new poetry that was enormously valuable, but
surely not as the sum total of possible artistic achievement.
Pound was acting as if he had invented "a wholly new aesthetic,"
and the movement had, "with *Poetry*'s help, progressed to the
point where it was taken seriously in some quarters at least."[6]
The insistent claims of the new movement were for a single-
minded approach to poetry, and Harriet Monroe was not willing
to grant Imagism the exclusive domain. What the Imagists needed
was a magazine of their own; and, with Pound's help, they finally
found it in the *New Freewoman,* which later became the famous
Egoist, under the direction of Richard Aldington and T. S. Eliot.

In May, 1915, Harriet Monroe refused to be the American
outlet for the *Egoist* edition of Imagist poetry, mainly because
she thought D. H. Lawrence's poetry indecent.[7] In a personal
letter to Miss Monroe, her associate editor Alice Corbin Hen-
derson wrote: "The need for perfectly fearless high standard
was never greater than it is at this moment. What we need to
do is to forget schools, forget Imagism, forget *vers libre* (now
that that's back history) and talk poetry."[8] Miss Monroe was
determined that *Poetry* was not going to be forced into the
position of a single-line defense of one esoteric poetic theory
over all others.

The battles of the Imagists transcended, of course, the pages
of *Poetry*; but the magazine continued to fire the controversy
by displaying the works of Pound, Aldington, H. D., Amy
Lowell, and others. To Miss Monroe, the conflict was healthy—

both for the poets and for the audience. She did not, however, forsake the new midwestern poets and continued to print poems by Sandburg and Masters, despite their obvious differences with Imagist theory. As we have observed, her personal preference was undeniably for American poetry which she felt was moving along dynamic lines.

Because *Poetry* favored, even if it did not endorse free verse, the magazine was frequently challenged by the *Dial*, its more conservative counterpart in Chicago. The *Dial* was troubled not only by the new freedom of verse form but more singularly by the absolute insistence on the poet's freedom of subject. Such poems as Sandburg's "Chicago Poems," Pound's "Tenzone," and several lyrics by D. H. Lawrence were the special objects of controversy. For the *Dial*, *Poetry* had robbed poetry of any possibilities for magic and for tragedy. In the *New Republic* and in *Poetry Journal*, Conrad Aiken also took the same line of protest: *Poetry* perpetrated a highly artificial and bloodless theory of poetry. But, despite some misgivings, Harriet Monroe refused to apologize for the contents of her magazine. For her, Imagism was "a healthy and vigorous movement, to be studied in its motives and principles, and its highest achievements, and not saddled with the weaknesses of its advocates or imitators."9

Even while the Imagist controversy ran high in the pages of the *Dial*, *Poetry* was making plans that were to establish it as the one magazine of international influence. It had always been Miss Monroe's desire not only to pay for the poetry which she actually printed but also to pioneer a campaign of prizes and awards comparable to those given in the fields of painting and sculpture. Unfortunately, this dream was never realized to its full extent; but the system of awards established in the first year of *Poetry's* existence has honored almost every major poet in modern American and British literature. In Miss Monroe's campaign to honor the poets, the first awards were made in November, 1913.

Poetry had had an exciting first year, and the contenders for the prize made a clear choice difficult. Pound strongly favored Yeats, who certainly was the most imposing figure of the group. But to give the award to a poet who was already internationally famous seemed, to Miss Monroe, rather "obvious and unadventurous." The decision, nevertheless, was made to award the first prize to Yeats for "The Grey Rock." This decision was a most fortunate one because it established both a standard of excellence and a sense of prestige for the prize. To receive the award once given to so great a poet had, for later poets, a very special quality of honor and achievement. In the most current listing of *Poetry*'s awards, the roll call of names from Yeats to the present attests to both the perceptive judgment and permanent quality of the poetry which has been so honored.

Discussion about the awarding of the first prize revealed Harriet Monroe's insistent desire to honor American poetry. While she concurred in the justness of the first prize for Yeats, she was reluctant to see Lindsay's "General Booth" go unhonored. She thus persuaded one of her benefactors to finance a second prize of one hundred dollars for the Lindsay poem. When "General Booth" had first appeared in the pages of *Poetry*, it had caused, as we have noted, a storm of conservative reaction; but it was exactly the kind of poetry which Miss Monroe hoped to foster in future issues. If *Poetry* could become a display place for such adventures in poetry, she would be encouraged because the presence of such poetry meant that poets themselves were seeking new solutions and were not depending on uninspired orthodoxy.

The whole system of annual awards for poetry also reflected Miss Monroe's attitude about the general failure of public recognition for the poet. As an art critic, she had been keenly aware of the glamour and attention bestowed upon paintings of questionable value; as a poet, her reaction to the neglect of her craft was understandable. The genuinely remarkable aspect of the system which she later instituted was, of course, its success. There is almost no way to indicate the quality of this success other than a listing of the poets whose work was so honored. But a list itself would be deceptive because it would fail to account for the crucial timeliness of the honor. To merely say that Eliot and Snodgrass are names in the list conveys nothing more than the fact that poets of great quality were recognized.

To recognize—and therefore to encourage—a young poet of talent and potential is the more difficult task. Thus, behind the roster of impressive names, we find an editorial sagacity unmatched by any other indicators of future poetic achievement.

Whatever later achievement was made by these individual poets, their early recognition by Harriet Monroe surely contributed its small part. Through the years, the list of awards by *Poetry* represents the work of many poets who only later achieved national and even international fame. *Poetry* has awarded honors to Carl Sandburg, Edgar Lee Masters, Wallace Stevens, Hart Crane, Amy Lowell, Marianne Moore, Robert Frost, Dylan Thomas, and to many other equally renowned poets. There were remarkably few mistakes in predicting the potential of the young poets.

A few months after *Poetry* had awarded prizes to Yeats and Lindsay for works which appeared in its pages, Rabindranath Tagore, whose work had also been featured in an early issue of the magazine, was awarded the 1913 Nobel Prize for Literature. *Poetry* had officially "discovered"—at least in English—this Asian poet whose name was then resounding throughout the world. "I drew a long breath of renewed power," Miss Monroe wrote, "and felt that my little magazine was fulfilling some of our seemingly extravagant hopes."[10]

The excitement of the first year was high: *Poetry* had printed many works of permanent quality, and the magazine was clearly estbalished. What had once been a mere dream now became a firm fact in Miss Monroe's life. She had succeeded to a position of persuasive power after long periods of disappointment and despair for poetry. Obviously, the magazine had now become the central point of her personal and professional career. *Poetry's* offices, a center of excitement, were visited by Rupert Brooke, Carl Sandburg, Vachel Lindsay, Robert Frost, and a host of other poets. What was new in poetry came first to *Poetry*; and, although Miss Monroe was herself never categorical, her judgment was influential in determining new directions for the art. Some might have caviled with her about individual poems, but none could deny the broad success of the magazine in providing both a new format and new energy for poetry.

II *World War I*

The brilliant beginning of the first year was soon marred by the international catastrophe of World War I. To Miss Monroe, the specter of war seemed to submerge all other interests; and she wondered whether her "little esthetic enterprise could keep its head up through the fiery flood."[11] The fear was only a passing depression; Miss Monroe was too firm of purpose to allow herself disproportionate reactions. In an editorial, printed in September, 1914, she encouraged the poet to strip the glamour from war and to portray its true and brutal aspects. In the same issue of *Poetry*, the editors announced plans for a special war number. To their great surprise, the magazine received over seven hundred entries for the special number. When the final fourteen poems for the issue were collected, they included works by Maxwell Bodenheim, Carl Sandburg, Amy Lowell, and Wallace Stevens, who was making his first appearance in *Poetry*. Throughout the years of strife, the editors continued to print poems of protest about war; and later issues featured poems by Rupert Brooke, Joyce Kilmer, Alan Seeger, D. H. Lawrence, and many others.

As the war years droned on, *Poetry* had its inevitable successes, despite the dispiriting national situation. From the vantage point of the 1970's, we realize how rapidly and diversely the new movements in modern poetry were developing in the crucial years following the founding of *Poetry*. The war itself had stimulated many poets to action, and *Poetry* was always receptive to their work. On both the American and British scene, many new poets were coming to the fore. The influence of T. E. Hulme and Ezra Pound had done much to give poetry and younger poets a different plan of attack, and the Whitmanian insistence on catholicity of subject matter had its influence. Those who insisted on writing in the old manner were being supplanted by poets who aggressively sought a more strident rhythm and who imposed that new music on all types of subjects. Throughout these early years—and this fact is especially true of the first five years of *Poetry*'s existence—*Poetry* was frequently the first periodical to print poems by men who were later to dominate their age in literature. Among such contributors were T. S. Eliot and Wallace Stevens, who made their first appearances in the pages of *Poetry*. Although the war years brought national sorrow—a spiritual depression reflected in the pages of *Poetry*—they were also years of many "discoveries."

Ralph Waldo Emerson once called his essays "jottings on the larger curve," a phrase suggesting the series or moments of intellectual excitement that are mere parts of a larger and more exciting mental universe. Like Emerson's "jottings," the pages of *Poetry* were individual moments of excitement within a larger artistic universe; for, often brilliant as small-scale, individual works of art, the many poems selected for the pages of the publication were beginning to coalesce into larger movements, to express a new temper and a new time. With space in *Poetry* the only limitation, Miss Monroe sought to give every poet of quality an opportunity to be heard. Despite her intention, the most frequent charge leveled against her magazine was that it purported to be little more than a trade organ, a place for displaying the wares of an industry; but a comparison of *Poetry* with such a publication does not sustain this adverse criticism.

That *Poetry* hoped to give the poet a chance to reach out to nourishing appreciation is attested to by the fact that during its first five years of existence, *Poetry* had printed scores of poems, whose uniqueness had come to define the essence of modern poetry. By 1917, the lines of "the larger curve" were more clearly definable when, in response to many inquiries and urgings, Miss Monroe and her first associate editor, Alice Corbin Henderson, compiled an anthology of twentieth-century verse, *The New Poetry*. Many of the poets and poems represented in the volume were drawn directly from the pages of *Poetry* itself, and the remarkable renascence of poetry which had taken place from 1912 to 1917 revealed how well *Poetry*'s editors had been attuned to the spirit of the revival. Indeed, the principles of selection for *The New Poetry* were the ones Miss Monroe had employed in selecting poetry for the pages of *Poetry*.

In the Introduction to the first edition of *The New Poetry*, Harriet Monroe recorded the distinguishing and essential elements of modern poetry. The details of form, she wrote, are not different; "for much poetry infused with the new spirit conforms to the old measures and rhyme-schemes."[12] The crucial differences are to be defined in the poet's commitment of his art to a more "immediate realization of life": "Thus inspired, it becomes objective. The term 'exteriority' has been applied to it, but this is incomplete. In presenting the concrete object or the concrete environment, whether these be beautiful or ugly, it seeks to give more precisely the emotion arising from them, and thus widens immeasurably the scope of the art."[13] The new poetry also possessed an "authentic vitality of theme" because it spoke from a direct relationship "with contemporary thought, contemporary imaginative and spiritual life." Writing in late 1916, Miss Monroe ascribed the emergence of "the new poetry" to the influence of two great Irish masters—John Millington Synge and William Butler Yeats. Recognizing that only time could give authority to such a statement of influence, she wished to record what seemed to her judgment the meaningful direction of contemporary poetry.

Like T. S. Eliot, Miss Monroe would have disclaimed any systematic and formal statement of poetic theory. Her poetic principles were, nevertheless, much firmer than would appear from a reading of the miscellaneous editorials which appeared every month in *Poetry*. Her own knowledge of poetry and the poets was, of course, extensive. Thus, when she compiled *The New Poetry*, she had already the knowledge and experience of five years of first-rate editorship at her command. As a result, the publication of *The New Poetry* was significant for a number of reasons: it signaled the emergence of a body of poetry that was both different and distinguished in its own right; furthermore, *The New Poetry* made modern verse available for study in colleges and universities. The literary historian was now enabled to assess the artistic contribution of a number of poets who seemed to be working in a more radical direction from the type of poetry acceptable to broad modern taste or to popular taste. The difference in the serious quality of *The New Poetry* was one of direction and modernity imposed by the judgment of Harriet Monroe. By rejecting poetry that failed to come to terms with modern life, she imposed an editorial value that helped determine the shape of modern poetry in America.

The first five years of *Poetry*'s existence were ones of intense excitement for a venture that many doubted could be sustained beyond a few brief, fitful issues. Along with *Poetry*, a great number of "little magazines" were shaping the literary milieu in 1912-17; each came into existence to combat a more or less clearly defined objective. In the total picture, we find a puzzling complexity and diversity of motive and intention behind the various periodicals. There were magazines whose editorial exclusiveness catered to leftist, regional, experimental, critical, and

eclectic interests. In defining the essence of the "little magazine,"
Frederick J. Hoffman has said that they are founded for two
reasons: rebellion against traditional modes of expression and
the wish to experiment with novel (and sometimes unintel-
ligible) forms; a desire to overcome the commercial or material
difficulties created by the introduction of any writing whose
commercial merits have not been proved.[14]

Unlike the many other little magazines which came into
existence in the early years of this century, *Poetry* survived
because of the power of its founder-editor. Certainly the motives
which Hoffman ascribes to the birth of the advance-guard
magazine were part of the impetus for *Poetry*. But *Poetry* did
not purport to serve any cause beyond the art of the poet;
it was not dominated by any special interest, nor was it confined
to the propagation of a specific poetic theory. Harriet Monroe
was able to sustain the excitement of the earliest issues because,
unlike other editors of some little magazines, she never lost
her central enthusiasm and concern for poetry.

The history of these first years of *Poetry* is entangled with
the names of many persons who helped the publication to
achieve its great success. These many friends of *Poetry* all had
an unflagging respect for Miss Monroe and for the task she
was performing for poetic art. The magazine could count many
successes to its credit; it had firmly established the "new poetry"
as a creative effort worthy of public attention and acclaim.
And, in spite of the contending claims for attention, Harriet
Monroe had steered a course of editorial direction that satisfied
her first objective—to serve the poet. *Poetry* was dominated by
her personality. In the hands of a less catholic editor, such
domination would have been fatal; but, in the case of *Poetry*,
it proved to be the single most important influence of its
continuing success.

III   *The Monroe-Pound Association*

The initial success and subsequent history of *Poetry* must
include a more detailed account of the important role which
Ezra Pound played in the early stages of the magazine. When
Miss Monroe had first invited Pound to be a contributor, she
was unaware of his unique position as a kind of poetic arbiter

for young and new poets, nor did she foresee that his special abilities would be invaluable to the project which she had so modestly begun. Pound's response to the invitation was decisive, enthusiastic, hopeful, and stimulating: "I am interested, and your scheme, as far as I understand it, seems not only sound, but the only possible method. There is no other magazine in America which is not an insult to the serious artist and to the dignity of his art." He also offered to make *Poetry* the exclusive American outlet for his work and, as we have noted, to be its foreign correspondent.

Miss Monroe foresaw the particular merit of the international connections that Pound, located in London, could bring to *Poetry* by procuring the works of young poets who might not have come to the attention of Miss Monroe in her distant Chicago base. Moreover, he was adamantly serious about the art of poetry, and he was full of lively and aggressive suggestions for *Poetry's* future.

Throughout the years during which they were associated, Pound and Monroe never met each other. With her care for detail, Miss Monroe preserved all of the Pound correspondence; but her own letters to him were not retained. Since she penned most of her correspondence, no carbon copies were filed for future reference. In order to construct an idea of their relationship, we are, therefore, dependent solely on Pound's letters which are preserved in the Harriet Monroe Collection at the University of Chicago. The very full Pound file suggests that a constant flow of communication passed between the two editors. Even in the earliest of Pound's letters, he quickly assumed the pattern of discussing editorial issues in an "our" or "we" fashion, and he assumed for himself an equal voice in shaping the content and editorial stance of the magazine.

Despite the wisdom and urgency with which Pound addressed himself to Miss Monroe, she was determined that he would not dominate *Poetry*. She certainly must have guessed that, if she were more permissive, Pound—clearly the more vocal personality—would eventually destroy *Poetry* by making it the sounding board for his immediate enthusiasm and by narrowing the scope of the magazine to the esoteric. Miss Monroe was primarily concerned with the acceptance and continuing success of *Poetry*, and Pound frequently seemed to be placing the

magazine in jeopardy by insisting upon impossibly high stand-
ards. There was, therefore, on her part, always a resistance
to many of Pound's proposals.

Essentially, the two editors differed about certain fundamental
objectives. Miss Monroe had conceived *Poetry* as a place where
the serious poet would meet with a generous and hospitable
reception; and, as noted earlier, she did not favor one form
of poetry over another, and did not conceive *Poetry* to be a
weapon in intellectual controversies. Her limitations were more
realistic: *Poetry* was not to be the voice of social culture or
to comment upon pressing human and political issues. As long
as she was editor, *Poetry* never assumed the role of shaping
the contemporary scene; instead, Miss Monroe hoped to *reflect*
that scene in the poetry of the age.

Even when Miss Monroe violently disagreed with the sub-
stance and ideas of specific poems, she generously printed the
work because a serious poet deserved the right to a hearing.
She was keenly conscious that great poetry must be ultimately
dependent on the richness of a social culture and that a developed
and sympathetic intellectual climate is itself the product of a
very diverse and subtle combination of forces. In Miss Monroe's
judgment, *Poetry* could not force its poetic evaluations upon
an unwilling public; it could only act as an educative force to
foster gently a more discriminating taste. In trying to achieve
these ends, Miss Monroe was inevitably motivated by a stern
pragmatism.

Pound concurred in these objectives, but his manner and
his method were more radical and imperative. He had a supreme
confidence in his own judgment, and he was always too ready
to damn any opposition as wrongheaded and aberrant opinion.
As early as January, 1913, he wrote: "We've simply GOT to
lead. Otherwise we sink to the level of a dozen other dilettante
ventures. We can't compete on business terms with the Home
Journal. We can't afford to give the public what it wants."[15]
But Miss Monroe knew that *Poetry* also could not afford to
alienate the public by offering poetry which merely offended.
Part of the contention which existed between the two editors
was, of course, traceable to the attitudes which each possessed
toward America itself. Miss Monroe, who was always optimistic
about the American scene, was by temperament more receptive

to the then-emerging American talent while Pound generally
denigrated it. In Pound's view, Lindsay as a poet was no match
for Hilda Doolittle or Aldington. Pound's letters to Miss Monroe
were numerous during this period and are incredibly spirited
ones, full of imperatives and urgent demands that *Poetry* stand
for excellence or nothing.

During late 1913 and early 1914, Pound worked indefatigably
for *Poetry*, procuring many poems that might not have otherwise
come to *Poetry*'s attention. These were years of "a great deal
more literary ferment" in London than in any American city,
and Pound generously channeled much of the new talent to
Poetry. These new poets' works were marked by a clarity of
new poetic purposes while young American poets were still
struggling in a dissatisfied way with their existing poetic forms
and ideas without being able to find a center for their emerging
talent. By encouraging the Imagist movement in the pages of
Poetry, Pound gave the magazine a shape and force it might
not otherwise have achieved if it had been left to its own
resources.

Moreover, Pound's effect on *Poetry* was bracing, and it no
doubt forced Miss Monroe—as time went on—to be more and
more selective in what she accepted for publication. There
were mistakes—such as John G. Neihardt's Roman tragedy—but
they were also educative ones; and Pound was ever ready to
use these errors of judgment to warn against being content
with a parochial standard. Pound urged the editor and her
associates to search for the serious, the master work, and to
entertain experiments only when they were promising and
serious. "You can't possibly," he wrote, "pat all the semi-defunct
on the head and be sincere." In his first letter to Miss Monroe,
Pound had asked: "Are you for American poetry or for poetry?
The latter is more important, but it is important that America
should boost the former, provided it doesn't mean a blindness
to the art. The glory of any nation is to produce art that can
be exported without disgrace to its origin."[16] In all his subsequent
correspondence, Pound stressed "the art of poetry" above any
other considerations. Pound was so insistent, and so frequently
critical, that Alice Corbin Henderson, the associate editor, soon
found his letters "depressing," perhaps because he was con-

ceding little to the difficult and intelligent efforts being made
in the home office.

Part of the difficulties of Miss Monroe with Pound were ones
that arose from the printing schedule of the magazine. As
Poetry's fame spread, it continued to receive an increasingly
larger selection of high-quality poetry. The editor tried to
establish some priorities in her printing schedule, and many
times she made written or verbal commitments about the pub-
lication of specific poems. Pound was at times unwilling to
honor the established schedule, a point which caused consider-
able stress for both the editor and Pound himself; for Pound
also needed to make printing commitments since much of the
material he was procuring for *Poetry* was by authors with some
reputation and stature whose work could be accepted with the
assurance that it would soon be published. Occasionally, Miss
Monroe's failure to honor Pound's promise or commitment placed
him in an embarrassing position; for he was forced to play a
delaying action. From his point of view, he was sending work
of the highest quality; therefore, the annoyance of being asked
to wait justly angered him. Pound recognized that he was per-
forming a very valuable service for the magazine, and he saw
no valid reason for not being given equal editorial responsibility
in determining the content of each issue.

Perhaps Pound appeared overzealous and dictatorial to Alice
Henderson, but it would be false to portray him as implacable
in his demands. He naturally had his own reasons for working
so assiduously to place young writers in print; and, during the
period that he and Miss Monroe were cooperating, he gave
Poetry the first opportunity for his "discoveries." "I may seem
a bit arbitrary," he wrote, "but I get stuff that no one else
could possibly get you. I do this by use, or abuse if you like,
of the privilege of personal friendship or acquaintance. If added
to that there is to be constant worry about dates of publication
etc. delays, etc. I simply can not go on with it, it is too wearing
to a set of nerves that have received few favors from circum-
stance. These people can't be treated like novices sending un-
invited contributions to *Harper's*."[17] In printing his own poetry,
he readily gave Miss Monroe the power of discretion to delete
or change his work; but he warned her not to "brandish the
blue pencil of decency until you have weighed the outrages

against the undercurrent of hygiene."[18] When other writers were concerned, he refused to permit either delays in printing or textual changes; for he maintained that every editor must respect the vision and integrity of the poem. An editor could refuse to print a poem, but he has no right to ask an author to Christianize his work.

Although Miss Monroe professed no personal religious convictions, she was strangely respectful of Christian attitudes. She preferred not to print poems which reflected an arch disregard for the Christian tradition. Perhaps she preferred not to offend needlessly in this respect, but her attitude was a point of nicety that frequently irritated Pound. "If one is trying to express," he wrote, "the passing of the gods, in poetry that expression is distinctly weakened by the omission of the one god or demi-god who is still popularly accepted."[19] While not disagreeing in substance, Miss Monroe may have merely been apprehensive about introducing such an emotional subject in *Poetry.*

The same kind of respect that she maintained for the accepted pattern of Christian belief also influenced other attitudes and subjects. In her mind, anything that exceeded some elusive bounds of decency was either tasteless or vulgar. Pound, of course, was considerably franker in his thinking, as his letters—replete with *damns* and *hells*—show. The whole problem of "indecency" for Miss Monroe was not a mere matter of personal dislike for poetry which in her mind transcended the socially acceptable; it also involved legal questions and the problems of censorship. Again, Miss Monroe was being highly protective about the magazine; and she was reluctant to become embroiled in defending the rights of authors to absolute free expression. Lawrence became a case in point for Miss Monroe and Pound. And, while Pound professed no special regard for D. H. Lawrence as a person, he valued his work as serious and as eminently artistic. In regard to Lawrence, Miss Monroe was influenced by her own prejudice; she never knowingly printed poetry which contained strong sexual overtones. She rejected several of Lawrence's poems because, in her view, they exceeded what she interpreted to be publicly acceptable standards of taste regarding sexual subject matter.

The same attitudes which prevailed on "Christianity" and

"decency" also had a strange extension in Miss Monroe's attitude
toward views about the future: Miss Monroe was exceedingly
intolerant of a defeatist attitude in poetry. She preferred always
to see life in more positive and fruitful terms, and poetry which
took an eminently negative view of life incurred her dislike.
When Pound first became acquainted with T. S. Eliot, he im-
mediately sensed Eliot's depth of talent and potential. Early
in October, 1914, he wrote to Harriet Monroe, enclosing "The
Love Song of J. Alfred Prufrock," and calling it "The most
interesting contribution I've had from an American."[20] The poem
failed to strike a similarly responsive chord from Miss Monroe;
she apparently objected to Pound that "Prufrock" was a debili-
tating character. Greatly annoyed, Pound replied that " 'Mr.
Prufrock' does not 'go off at the end.' It is a portrait of failure,
or of a character which fails, and it would be false to make
it end on a note of triumph . . . a portrait satire on futility can't
end by turning that quintessence of futility, Mr. P. into a re-
formed character breathing out fire and ozone."[21] In spite of
Pound's firm endorsement, Miss Monroe continued to temporize;
but she finally published Eliot's poem in June, 1915.

The striking differences of attitude were not always resolved,
however, to the mutual satisfaction of either Pound or Miss
Monroe. According to her best light, Miss Monroe was trying
to secure the future of *Poetry*. If the magazine were to be a
sustaining institution, she recognized that it could not be wholly
partisan; it could not afford to reject the serious efforts of
established or promising poets because their work did not meet
Pound's manifesto for "modern" poetry. One genuine flaw in
Miss Monroe's editorial judgment, however, was her inability
to separate the value of an idea expressed in poetry from the
value of poetry as poetry. Because of personal bias, she was,
for example, as noted, less receptive to poetry which was critical
of Christian or American culture. No respecter of these social
institutions, Pound was perhaps more catholic than Miss Monroe.

Throughout 1913, Pound was extremely active not only in
procuring contributions from poets who have since become
international figures but in securing a number of critical essays,
and he encouraged Miss Monroe to expand *Poetry* to include
first-rate criticism. One of the finest of the early critical articles
which *Poetry* printed was Ford Madox Ford's essay, "Impres-

sionism," which Pound had secured for the magazine, but with which he again had some difficulty in the printing schedule. Pound was moving in many directions, and the poetry and prose which he was submitting for publication in *Poetry* may have seemed to the founder-editor to be impinging upon her freedom of choice; particularly since, as we have noted, the poets whom she chose to print seldom met with Pound's approval.

At the time, Pound was egocentric enough to believe that Miss Monroe was not adequately prepared to perform her critical task. In November, 1913, he tendered his resignation as foreign correspondent; in the same month, he referred to Miss Monroe in a letter to Amy Lowell as "a bloody fool" and expressed his hope that he was "shed of the bloomin' paper."[22] With some diplomacy, Miss Monroe convinced him that, despite differences of critical judgment, his efforts for *Poetry* were deeply valued. As an outlet for many of his literary activities, *Poetry* was still useful to Pound; and he continued to act as its foreign correspondent until 1917.

In late 1913, Pound's energies were soon diverted from *Poetry* when he secured a firmer position in the editorial control of the *New Freewoman*, which later became the *Egoist*. At this stage, Pound's interest in Imagism was at its height; and he regarded the new periodical as a purer medium than *Poetry* for the poets whose work he admired and wished to promote. Thus, he was soon dividing his energies; and, because Miss Monroe was proving recalcitrant, Pound favored the *New Freewoman*. Pound was also involved in compiling material for *Les Imagistes,* which was published in March, 1914, and which he hoped would prove to be a definitive practical guide to Imagism.

But dissension soon arose among the contributors to Pound's anthology; and Amy Lowell, now fully imbued with Imagist principles, determined to publish an anthology covering very much the same poetic ground and using the word "Imagism" in the title. As the first promoter and titular head of Imagism, Pound refused to have his name associated with an anthology over which he could not cast his imprimatur. When Miss Lowell convinced the small band of poets whom Pound had first encouraged to follow her lead, Pound considered the whole movement perverted to "Amygism." As K. L. Goodwin has observed:

"The shock of the Imagists' defection seems to have made Pound somewhat disgruntled about his campaigns to help young writers, and to have suggested to him that he might devote more time to his own 'actual creation.' "[23]

When Pound had removed himself from the Imagist poets residing in London, *Poetry*, of course, featured less and less of their work, although both Pound and Amy Lowell continued to print a good deal of their new work in the pages of *Poetry*. Still acting as foreign correspondent, but without the initial fervor that marked his first two years of service, Pound continued to offer new poetry that came his way to Miss Monroe; she was, for example, the first to print the poetry of James Joyce in this country.

Pound's greatest contribution to poetry and to *Poetry* was the decisive and lasting influence which he exerted on Imagism. "Without him," Goodwin comments, "it is almost certain that Imagism would never have become a movement. He provided the energy that got the creative works and the critical principles published; he gave the movement a name; and his publicity secured for it a degree of fame or notoriety."[24] Because of Pound's position as a literary promoter in 1912-14, *Poetry* gained an inestimable advantage. Almost immediately, *Poetry* gave the American scene a viable alternative; and its sole championship of Imagism was the incitement for much experimenting and innovation. While Pound's and Miss Monroe's working relationship was operating well, they succeeded in changing the literary atmosphere. Without Pound, it is doubtful if Miss Monroe would have had the courage to be so daring in those early issues; indeed, *Poetry* stood alone in those days in its advanced endorsement of a radical direction for art.

Although Pound had turned from the Imagist movement after mid-1914, he continued to have a more sporadic relationship with *Poetry* until 1919, when his name was officially removed from the roster of editors. The poets whom Pound had introduced—H. D., Aldington, Yeats, Lawrence, Frost, and Ford Madox Ford—continued to contribute their works. The effect of Pound's growing estrangement from *Poetry* was not noticeable, therefore, in the kind or quality of work which continued to appear in the magazine. A recent critic of Pound has claimed for the poet that he "inspired and led critical interest in modern poetry in the United States."[25] No such claim can be maintained, however, without due credit to *Poetry* and to Harriet Monroe.

IV   *Poetry's Editorial Policy to the 1930's*

In 1962, *Poetry* celebrated its fiftieth anniversary, an event which distinguished the magazine from almost any other "little magazine." Of the many "little magazines" which began publication in the second decade of this century, only *Poetry* has survived as a clear testament to the acute editorial skill of its founder-editor. But to be distinguished by the mere fact of survival in the dubious and competitive world of the "little magazine" would be an empty tribute were not *Poetry* equally distinguished as the one magazine in America which has discovered and brought forth what can now only be regarded as a fantastic array of poetic greatness.

Harriet Monroe, its founder-editor, possessed, as we have noted, a unique wisdom and pragmatism which guided the magazine through the difficult days of its inception and established a pattern of editorial stability that allowed the magazine to sustain itself and to surmount the problems that were usually fatal to the ventures of "little magazines." Many commentators have remarked that every editor brings the unique traits of his personality to bear upon the magazine which he edits. For example, the violence of such a magazine as *Blast* was a clear extension of the preoccupations of Wyndham Lewis, and its bold type and urgency are also found in much of Lewis' later writings. To sustain the heat which *Blast* generated could have proceeded only from a man of Lewis' temperament—unpredictable and urgent; but Lewis was directing his energies at many nebulous and unspecified ills in the literary and social community. In the end, he was destructive; and nothing viable emerged from the combative efforts of *Blast*. Another example of the editor's determining the quality of a periodical would, of course, be Margaret Anderson, the founder of the *Little Review*.

Unlike the editor of the *Little Review*, Miss Monroe was never the kind of person to become enthusiastically enraptured in anything; all of her actions were motivated by more stable standards. A mature woman of fifty-two when *Poetry* was

launched, Miss Monroe never suffered, as did Margaret Ander-
son, from erratic spells of enthusiasm: indeed, just as "Margaret
was volatile," as Bernard Duffey has stated, "unpredictable,
brilliantly imaginative, impatient, stubborn, [so] Harriet was
mature, serene, intelligent, and determined."[26] Such qualities of
personality were firmly imprinted on the character of the maga-
zine each woman edited. Of prime importance to the survival
of *Poetry* was the quality of stability, which had its source in
the strength of Miss Monroe.

When examining the issues of *Poetry* from 1912 to 1936, we
are immediately impressed by the diversity represented in its
pages. Interspersed among the poems bearing the names of
Ernest Hemingway, W. H. Auden, T. S. Eliot, John Crowe
Ransom, Richard P. Blackmur, Joseph Warren Beach, and Robert
Penn Warren are those of less well-known and recognizable
poets. Some of these unknown figures appear only once, or
their poems appear over a few months or years and then are
seen no more. Because no editor can discern what talents may
survive, the casual observer might conclude that *Poetry* lacked
the fine discrimination to separate the master work from the
merely sporadic and spurious.

About *Poetry*'s diversity, Horace Gregory has commented:
"Read swiftly and without discrimination it would seem that the
secret of *Poetry*'s editorial selection of verse was to have no
policy at all."[27] As a judgment about the magazine's policy,
the comment provokes a singularly important question: Was
the magazine guided by a concrete editorial policy that was
ultimately responsible for its literary success? The question
admits of no easy answer, and perhaps it can never be answered
to the complete satisfaction of all of the magazine's critics.
Among *Poetry*'s critics, there is no doubt that Harriet Monroe
was the one person responsible for adroitly maneuvering her
magazine into a position of influence and greatness. To gauge
the success of *Poetry*, we must explore the personality behind
the policy.

The two words most frequently used to describe *Poetry*'s
editorial policy are "eclectic" and "catholic." As descriptive
terms, they may be interpreted as vices or virtues, depending
on the individual critic. Horace Gregory has praised the maga-
zine for its inclusive sweep and ability to cut across all lines

of poetic differences: "Eclecticism was the very life of the magazine and within it one may find the evidence of Miss Monroe's cultural heritage."[28] As Gregory assessed *Poetry*'s editorial success, he found it to consist in discovering the best poetry in many types and styles; he attributed to the magazine an intelligent overview of the field, a policy which enabled the editors to select the best of diverse strains in modern poetry. On the same point, Pound has written: "An exclusive editorial policy would not have done the work of an inclusive policy.... It is to Miss Monroe's credit that *Poetry* never degenerated into a factual organ."[29] The inclusiveness which Pound praises as a virtue was earlier a policy that he had, however, violently challenged. In 1926, he wrote: "My impression is that you have tried ladies' numbers, children's numbers, in fact everything but a man's number. And that you tend to become more and more a tea party, all *mères de famille*, only one fallen woman among them (and 'er with the sob of repentance)."[30] In the perspective of 1936—long after Pound had severed his connection with *Poetry*—he came to appreciate the more obvious value of the magazine's inclusive policy and the firm determination on Harriet Monroe's part to keep *Poetry* above factionalism which was always self-defeating.

In celebrating its fiftieth anniversary, Henry Rago, then the editor of *Poetry,* returned once again to the magazine's long editorial commitment to inclusiveness. In his commentary he preferred to characterize the magazine's policy as "catholic" rather than as "eclectic" because of this word's connotation of selecting and choosing "parts." Instead, Rago thought of *Poetry* as essentially hospitable to all forms of serious poetry; and this assessment of the function of *Poetry* more aptly catches the spirit of the magazine as Harriet Monroe had guided its policy. If she was occasionally unsympathetic to some forms of poetry, she was never inhospitable.

When Horace Gregory wrote that the secret of *Poetry*'s selection of verse seemed not to depend upon any discernible principles, he was questioning not only the concreteness of the magazine's policy but also its basic liberalism. That Miss Monroe was truly liberal in spirit occasioned little argument among her critics. When she founded *Poetry*, it was with the spirit of liberalism that was willing to assay both sides of a question.

For this trait of her character, Pound has paid her the finest tribute: "The elasticity of her perceptions and the freshness of her interests were those of a great editor, and as no one more acrimoniously differed with her in point of view than I did, I think no one is better able to testify to her unfailing purity of her intentions."[31] It was "the freshness of her interests" which gave the magazine its quality of diversity.

This inclusiveness was intended from the first. In the second issue of *Poetry*, Miss Monroe declared: "The Open Door will be the policy of this magazine—may the great poet we are looking for never find it shut, or half-shut, against his ample genius! To this end the editors hope to keep free of entangling alliances with any single class or school. They desire to print the best English verse which is being written today, regardless of where, by whom or under what theory of art it is written. Nor will the magazine promise to limit its editorial comments to one set of opinions."[32] Miss Monroe was convinced, as we have noted before, that the growth and development of genius could never be an isolated process; and, had the magazine restricted itself to a limited theory of poetry or to poetry informed by a special advocacy for ideas, the chance of discovering the great poets would be severely minimized. "Since 'The Masterpiece' is always a rarity, and it blooms not in the desert, but in the midst of lesser growth,"[33] isolation and exclusivity were, for her, self-defeating policies; and she encouraged a healthy pluralism in the subjects and forms of poetry. In its search for great poets, the magazine printed, as we have observed, a good deal of "lesser growth" and thereby quite naturally created controversy; but Miss Monroe believed that controversy was good for the soul and that the magazine which expressed but one opinion was doomed.[34]

From time to time, *Poetry*'s enemies accused the magazine of failure to realize its own ideals. Conrad Aiken and Ezra Pound were intensely critical of *Poetry*'s supposed restrictive attitudes, especially in the 1920's. A former associate editor and later the editor after Harriet Monroe's death, Jessica Nelson North, defended the magazine's policies: if the magazine did not always achieve the ideal which it had set for itself, if it was not so eclectic as it might have been, its policy was always extremely sincere.[35] Harriet Monroe herself also had the feeling that the magazine did not always produce the best work. "No doubt," she wrote, "we have compromised, we have followed false gods, we have kept our eyes on the ground, and have strayed into narrow places, and have been contented with little."[36] The statement is, of course, much too self-effacing; on the whole, Miss Monroe thought that the magazine had achieved a good record for printing the best that was being written at the time.

During Pound's tenure with *Poetry*, he would have agreed: "Now *Poetry* has frankly tried to widen the poet's range, to question conventional barriers, whether technical or spiritual, inherited from the past, and to help to bring the modern poet face to face with the modern world. We have printed not only odes and sonnets, blank verse drama, and rhymed pentameter narratives, but imagistic fugues, fantasies in *vers libre*, rhapsodies in polyphonic prose—any dash for freedom which seemed to have life in it—a fervor for movement and the beauty of open spaces—even if the goal was vague and remote, or quite unattainable in the distance."[37] Perhaps Pound tended to dramatize the situation, but his words reflect the facts. In a backward glance, Frederick Hoffman has assayed *Poetry*'s attitude toward experimentation and innovation much more soberly: "One of the values of *Poetry*'s early years was its hospitality to and its vigorous defense of experimentation in verse."[38]

That Miss Monroe was inclined to embrace a radical point of view about poetry may be seen in the many editorials which she wrote over the years and, in a more muted way, in her own poetry. But her radicalism was—as her poetry indicates—always of a very sober sort. In the Preface to the first edition of *The New Poetry*, she declared that, "As part of a movement, even the most extravagant experiments, the most radical innovations are valuable, for the moment at least, as an assault against prejudice."[39] Miss Monroe was well aware of the transitory value of "extravagant experiments"; she was also cognizant of the fact that anything which fostered extremes was essentially unworthy as art. This point of view had later ramifications in Miss Monroe's opposition toward Pound's encouragement toward total freedom in poetic form and content. As might be expected, while Harriet Monroe admitted the merit of Pound's radicalism, she never endorsed it with full sympathy. For her, the arch-enemy of poetry was complacency; but the solution to the dilemma of poetical inaction was not—as it had been for Margaret Anderson—extreme radicalism.

From the perspective of the early 1970's, much of the avant-garde literature of the earlier decades now appears as a less spectacular affront to convention or custom. Although *Poetry*, in the early years of its existence, was severely criticized by the conservative *Dial* as bizarre, astonishing, and even shocking, the liberalism of *Poetry* is more moderately assessed by Morton D. Zabel, who succeeded Harriet Monroe as editor.[40] In his tribute to *Poetry*, he ascribes its success to the editorial firmness which adjusted the claims of freedom and integrity with the equally insistent claims of moderation and sane restraint. *Poetry* "has been safely eclectic because it was stably personal; it has been sanely cosmopolitan because it has been so honestly native. If, in this adaptability to the conditions and confusions of one of poetry's most baffling periods, it has sometimes fallen in grace, it has never lost its sense of tradition, of standards, and authority."[41]

What Miss Monroe most admired in poetry was the spirit of adventure and originality—but, as we have noted, she did impose such limitations, such as those in regard to decency. In her estimation, "the most dangerous enemy of this spirit is self-distrust—a certain colonialism which leans upon London, Paris, New York, thus bidding our artists imitate instead of create, or exiling them instead of keeping them at home. Every artistic venture confronts the benumbing influence of this enemy, meets the facile temptation to become colonial."[42] In Miss Monroe's judgment, the terms "colonial," "esoteric," and "insular" were equally disparaging.

It is difficult to generalize about *Poetry*'s policy of accepting poems without restriction as to their form or content. While the magazine was always willing to accept poems of high quality, certain restrictions were inevitable; but these strictures were not a clearly defined part of the editorial policy as declared in the first issue; they came into being only as certain problems arose which seemed to Miss Monroe to be carrying modern poetry away from the important elements of art. The implementation of *Poetry*'s editorial policy obviously devolved upon the sensitive personal judgment of the first readers and, of course, ultimately upon Miss Monroe's poetic discretion and final acceptance of any poem for inclusion in the magazine. Another difficulty in assaying *Poetry*'s liberalism is the fact that there can be no opportunity to see and judge the poems which were rejected as unsuitable. We are forced, therefore, to judge the latitude of freedom given to the poet from those poems which the magazine actually printed and, of course, from the sporadic editorial comments on the subject.

In the "poet's circular," Miss Monroe had promised "to refuse nothing because it is too good, whatever the nature of its excellence. We shall read with special interest poems of modern significance, but the most classic subject will not be declined if it reaches a high standard of quality."[43] While *Poetry* militated against the evils of tradition, it also recognized the value of trusting to tradition; as a result, the magazine was never against traditional poems per se. "The great poets of today," wrote Miss Monroe, "do not discard tradition because they follow the speech of today rather than that of Shakespeare's time, or strive for organic rhythm rather than use a mold which has been perfected by others."[44] Following the lines set down by the poets of earlier centuries was uninspiring and imitative; the important thing to be learned from tradition was not the rules of prosody but the basic concepts of life and the cultural development reflected in the poetry. Of the modern poets, Miss Monroe asserted that "they follow the great tradition where they seek a vehicle suited to their own epoch and their own creative mood, and resolutely reject all others."[45]

The poetic revolution of 1912-19 produced a wide array of experiments in form. That *Poetry*'s policy was extremely receptive to these innovations is without question—as even a cursory examination of the early issues of the magazine proves. *Poetry*'s liberal attitude toward form produced some of the magazine's most stimulating controversies: the attacks on the free-verse movement, which *Poetry* championed as a new development in poetical freedom, were incited by its liberalism toward poetical form. When, in the early years, *Poetry*'s critics frequently belabored the magazine for printing works whose form was out of the mainstream of convention, Miss Monroe replied, "Most critics get used to one kind of movement; the wave as it recedes, leaves them high and dry—No, high and very damp; the next

wave bowls them over, and gets into their eyes and ears."[46]
If a poetic experiment possessed a unique integrity, if it seemed
serious and promising, the editors of *Poetry* were willing to
print the poem. What they hoped to guard against were poems
that were merely "formless moderne" or one that were only
linguistic novelties.

If the magazine was more liberal than its counterparts in
allowing every serious poetic form to prove its worth in the
arena of public opinion, the policy was due to the editor's firm
conviction that diversity of presentation was also the life of the
magazine. And if, at times, the reading public disagreed with
the editors' estimate of the poems which it printed, Miss Monroe
considered that to be a good sign. As Pound observed, "If one
is going to print opinions that the public already agrees with,
what is the use of printing 'em at all? Good art can't possibly
be palatable all at once."[47] If *Poetry* had confined itself to the
long-respected opinions and established meters, its function as
a stimulus to innovation and creative originality would have
ceased to exist.

In order to accommodate various kinds of poetry which had
either a special interest or a limited appeal, *Poetry* inaugurated
the practice of devoting single issues or numbers to poems of
distinct appeal. The practice itself was a stroke of editorial
genius because it allowed the magazine to expand beyond the
American-English tradition and to publish some of the best
work originating on a wider cultural scale. As a result of such
special issues, *Poetry* was able to feature exclusively the poetry
of India or Japan or to publish poetry with a distinct regional
cast, such as that in the Southwest issue. Within the limits of
the plan, *Poetry* afforded space to a type of poetry that, because
it did not cut across the broader range of poetic interest, had
unique merit in its own right. The editorial pattern of issuing
special numbers also afforded Miss Monroe the opportunity to
print the work of poets who were working in a similar vein or
who were loosely confederated into a "school."

While *Poetry* always tried to print representative works, Miss
Monroe was keenly aware of certain groups of poets whose
poetry expressed very definite ideas or poetical techniques. In
her judgment, it was never wise to devote endless pages to
these specialists. It became, therefore, the standard policy of

the magazine to allow these "schools" to be represented in single issues; thus, a coterie or group was given the advantage of displaying its best poems in a representative collection. In this way, Miss Monroe also hoped to avoid any confusion on the part of the reader or critic that *Poetry* advocated either the views expressed or the poetic form. Despite the concern of the editor to make these "special" issues appear as unique expressions of a kind of poetry—a poetry with its own sense of time and place—*Poetry* was often the object of either parody or one-sided critical jibes. When a special issue featured such poets as Allen Tate, Yvor Winters, and E. E. Cummings, an incensed reader wrote the following cancellation:

> My Money
>   is what i want
>   you heard me . . . money
> you got it
>   and i got poetry
> which, metaphorically speaking, is
> nothing but horsehair and metal discs in a Bach
>   fugue . . .
> my money, my money, my money

On another such occasion, Ezra Pound's poem, "Tenzone," was spoofed under the new title "Spring on State St."

> Will people accept them?
>   (i.e. these bargains)
> O dainty colorings and range of prices!
> Gowns of charmeuse in all
>   The colors of the seasons
> Blouse skirts of Russian cloth
>   Tucked belt of softest satin
> And only $37.50

That *Poetry* aspired to be unprejudiced and impersonal with regard to the intellectual content of the poems submitted for publication was part of its original policy; but, in the tenuous decision-making process of inclusion or exclusion, the liberal intent of the original policy was at times obscured by elements of style or content, which in the judgment of the founder-editor, detracted from the quality of the poem.

V   *Changing Editorial Views*

While the magazine was dedicated to free thought in prin-
ciple, its practice and theory did not always harmonize. The
spirit of confidence and affirmation which was so much a part
of Harriet Monroe's early life lingered as a continual influence
upon her attitudes toward the future which she hoped was
shaping the twentieth century. Her optimism was Emersonian
in its broad confidence of the greatness to be realized; but,
intellectually, she lagged behind the spirit of the 1920's and
1930's. Because she interpreted the cultural impress of these
two decades differently, she refused to believe that the poets
speaking in those years were accurately reflecting the spirit of
the times. Rather, she preferred to believe that their work was
aberrant, that it was inverted without honest purpose, and that
its convoluted language was only esoteric ornament. She resisted
the new poetry as a false voice of despiritualization; and she
simply found it impossible to believe in a less pleasant world
view.

These were serious limitations for one in so powerful a posi-
tion. Indeed, the magazine missed printing much fine poetry
because she was frankly prejudiced in her views. In gauging
the founder-editor's special influence, Frederick J. Hoffman
wrote: "There was little enough quarrel with Harriet Monroe,
except on the grounds that her editorial scrutiny had been at
times a bit austere and that she sometimes interfered with the
poet's right to 'absolute freedom' of expression."[48]

As we have indicated, her dislike of certain attitudes and
philosophies of life prevented her from accepting the works
of some poets who expressed these beliefs openly in their poems,
particularly works by the proletarian poets of the early 1930's.
An associate editor during this period, Jessica Nelson North
later observed that "the 'proletarian' poetry of the Thirties was
sometimes published in the magazine, but to a considerable
extent so was much lyric poetry of a 'softer' strain. I was quite
out of sympathy with the Marxian poets, and so was Harriet."[49]
It is interesting to note that *Poetry* did not print the more
characteristic work of Auden and Spender in the 1930's when
the center of their interest was on social reform. Even the
reviews of Auden's early work were reserved and unsympathetic.

During the late period of Miss Monroe's editorship, she came to be considered, in many quarters, as increasingly conservative. Some of *Poetry*'s critics thought that the magazine had changed course and had veered to a more conservative position in the 1930's—and, to a certain extent, this view was not incorrect. Since Miss Monroe was out of sympathy with the Marxian or class-conscious poets who were then prominent, she rarely printed their work. She had little respect for such new poets as Hart Crane, Allen Tate, Yvor Winters, Laura Riding, and others who followed their lead.[50] *Poetry*, however, printed their work because Miss Monroe, true to her principles, felt that these poets were serious and had a right to be heard.[51]

She was also not without strong reactions to certain other issues. That she admired poetry which expressed the immensity and vibrant life of modern culture was surely not a limitation; and, as a matter of fact, her optimistic philosophy of world progress was the foundation for her regard for some modern poets. But this unbounded optimism produced in her an acute dislike, as we have already observed, for pessimism or defeatism. While *Poetry* was dedicated to expressing all intellectual attitudes, it was never, at least under Miss Monroe's editorship, wholly sympathetic to much of the poetry produced in the wake of T. S. Eliot's *The Waste Land*. It is also interesting to note, in relation to this attitude of Miss Monroe, that *Poetry* never printed a single poem by either Thomas Hardy or A. E. Housman, although both men lived and wrote for many years after its founding.

Indeed, the early impulses and enthusiasms that had attended the founding of her magazine had begun to change their temper soon after World War I, as Horace Gregory has observed:

It would not be too far-fetched to say that the "poetic renaissance" came to a final conclusion with the publication of T. S. Eliot's poem, "The Waste Land," in the November 1922, issue of the *Dial*. From that moment onward, Harriet Monroe's position seemed to represent all the fervor, the warmth, the native quickness and innocence that defined the hopeful attitudes of Middle Western America before the war, and readers of "The Waste Land" became aware of something from another world than that of the "new" poetry of which Miss Monroe was so ardent a champion. The unrest and the spiritual malady that had become prevalent in the large cities of Europe and of the United States seemed to speak out in voices so disturbing that it was no longer possible to ignore them, and another day beyond the period of the "poetic renaissance" had well begun.[52]

Poetry was never able to re-create those exciting days of its early existence—the days of discovering poets such as Lindsay, Masters, and Sandburg.

The intellectual milieu had, indeed, changed; and every serious critic of *Poetry* admits that the magazine suffered because of it. Miss Monroe herself, sharply aware of the change in the literary climate, sensed portentous signs of poetry's future in Eliot's poem: "I have spoken," she editorialized, "of Eliot's 'Waste Land,' which gives a vivid suggestion of the whole vast modern fabric crashing down in ruinous chaos; and there are many other poems which present or imply or prophesy failure or spiritual disaster in the modern scheme. In other words, the poets have preferred weakness to strength. When mighty deeds are being done, they follow imaginatively not the hero who is doing but the underdog, be he labor-slave or highbrow, who is crushed by them."[53] After the publication of Eliot's highly influential poem, *Poetry* continued for some time to receive many poems imitative of Eliot's masterpiece. Dejected young men were writing about "rats and bones and crawling things" without understanding the basic integration with which they were utilized in *The Waste Land,* and Miss Monroe's attitude toward such disintegration was predictably hostile. It would, however, be wrong to conclude that *Poetry* restricted itself only to poems which reflected the world in a rosy light; the issues were not so sharply drawn, and all shades of poetic, religious and political philosophies are found in the pages of *Poetry.* If a poet could give voice and shape to an idea with style, delicacy, subtlety, and grace, Miss Monroe accepted the work.

VI   *Process of Selection*

The complex fabric of artistic judgments which ultimately composed the tenets of *Poetry*'s acceptance policy can never be isolated into a series of clear propositions. The process of acceptance must necessarily be seen in the context of individual poems. To attempt to separate this context from a consideration

of the issues of poetic technique produces an unfair impression
of the method which *Poetry* developed in analyzing a particular
poem. *Poetry* had one test, one method of evaluation, which
the editors applied to a poem; but this test involved corporate
artistic judgments.

According to Miss Monroe, the one test of acceptance for
any poem to be printed in *Poetry* was the quality of the work:
"The test, limited by ever-fallible human judgment, is to be
quality alone; all forms, whether narrative, dramatic or lyric,
will be acceptable."[54] As the decisive test, Miss Monroe could
not have selected a more nebulous critical word than "quality";
and the meaning which she attached to it is both vague and
equivocal. The exact criteria for evaluating a poem was, in
part, obviously dependent upon the impressionistic critical fac-
ulty of the editor or associate editors and therefore changed
from time to time—but the result was consistent: the magazine
consistently maintained a high standard of criticism, and it did
print many poems of permanent literary value.

Although Miss Monroe was the final judge of what the maga-
zine printed, she was rarely the first reader of the incoming
manuscripts, a task which was usually assigned by her to the
associate editors. Difficult and exhausting, the first reading
was to a large extent the most important in the tenuous process.
The enormity of the task becomes apparent when we realize
that *Poetry* received approximately five thousand manuscripts
each month. From this wealth of material, the editors could
print only twenty-five poems. Needless to say, Miss Monroe
always selected the most discriminating of her associates for
the position of first reader.

Almost without variation, the first readers were associated
with the editorial staff, and they usually rose to their position
after a period of critical apprenticeship, a time in which to
establish both trust and critical rapport. The first reader had
to be mature, alert, and sensitive; and he had to be able to
maintain a sharp sense of criticism over extended periods of
time. The first reader was responsible for eliminating all of the
poems which were trite and banal in thought, as well as those
which were poorly executed. Had the process been one merely
of elimination, the first reader's responsibility would have been
greatly simplified; but his task was more than just sorting the

wheat from the chaff. Up to a certain point, it was not too dif-
ficult to eliminate a large body of the incoming manuscripts—
those poems which were patently amateur and formlessly modern;
but, once through the first round of eliminations, there still re-
mained a large number of very good poems; and this group gave
the editors the most difficulty. Moreover, "It was here," as
Jessica Nelson North indicates, "that the personal prejudices of
the editors were most likely to make the decision."[55]

After the first readers had selected the most promising poems,
they submitted them to Miss Monroe for her final decision.
Generally, Miss Monroe sought the advice and criticism of others
before she rendered her final judgment. Since *Poetry's* offices
were a mecca for visitors—poets and other men of letters—Miss
Monroe often sought the opinions of her visitors about poems
being considered. Ironically, she would have already made her
own decision on the poem; and she rarely, if ever, changed her
mind, no matter what the visitor said about the work. Miss
Monroe was primarily interested in the visitor's reaction to the
poem; hence, whatever he said, either for or against the poem,
made no difference. Frequently, there was intraoffice dissension
over the merits of a particular poem; but Miss Monroe's decision
was usually final.

The crucial process of selection was, therefore, ultimately
subjective and dependent upon the discriminating taste of the
editors. For the period of Miss Monroe's editorial tenure, the
temper and tone of the magazine largely reflected her critical
attitudes. As Horace Gregory observed: "Harriet had put her
trust in the resources of her own imagination and intuition, and
since she also possessed the gift of common sense—that rarest of
all human senses—she made few mistakes in feeling and judg-
ment."[56] If the magazine failed at times to achieve the highest
standard of its own ideal, the sincerity and honesty of its editors
can never be doubted. As an editor, Miss Monroe did not feel
that she was choosing poems for all time; she viewed *Poetry* as
analogous to a fine-art center in which she, as editor, was hanging
up the best contemporary works for display. An error in judg-
ment was, therefore, less severe since she entertained no pre-
tension of printing only those poems of permanent significance.

Although we concede that *Poetry's* process of selection was a
combination of some definable critical criteria and a more

nebulous impressionistic reaction, we find it difficult to examine the final factors of taste which were so crucial to the process itself. However, as an aid to selecting good poems, Miss Monroe devised a set of guidelines or rules which could be applied to poems. Strictly speaking, these rules were not composed as critical touchstones for the editors or first readers; their chief purpose was to give the poets whose work was rejected some indication of the reason for the failure of their poems. In this context, the rules present a negative approach to the question of poetic quality, but they also illustrate what the magazine would not accept.

The following list is by no means complete, but it is a digest of the major points which were, according to Miss Monroe, the chief errors of the poets who submitted unacceptable verse:[57]

1. Any poem noticeably imitative of a known writer was taboo.

2. Structure was stressed. That is, the editors disliked poems which ran to great length and said too little.

3. Padding of lines to make them fit the rhythm was never accepted.

4. Any poeticesius, such as "winged" for "flew," "bloom" for "flower," "blue" for "sky," were usually rejected.

5. Propaganda poetry per se was never acceptable.

6. There was an editorial prejudice against overstatement; understatement was always better form.

7. There was a prejudice against typographical idiosyncrasies.

8. Personal verse or verse in dubious taste was unacceptable,

9. Language must be like heightened conversation unless the work was a period piece or gained atmosphere depending upon period words; otherwise, the poem had to be part of the modern age.

While these rules do not form a complete statement of the component factors in judging a poem, they serve to illustrate the objective side of the process. The subjective part, or the decisions which involved taste more than observable poetic technique, cannot be so easily demonstrated. A great deal of theoretical criticism has been written in attempts to define the perfect critic; but, despite the complexities of the individual theories, estheticians have ultimately been forced to rely upon the nebulous quality of taste. Eliot's concept of the ideal critic as one imbued with a structure of perceptions and a mature or developed sensibility are applicable to the critical taste of Miss Monroe. It is perfectly conceivable that *Poetry* received thousands of poems that did not violate the prejudices and rules established by the chief editor and her co-workers; yet, of these thousands, many, many were rejected for reasons that are today unassignable, except to the editor's individual sensibility and taste. In her long years of editorship, Miss Monroe was clearly in a position to acquire and exert the esthetic demands that Eliot placed upon the ideal critic; and she succeeded to an admirable degree. As the poetic revolution expanded and reached more and more diverse proportions, *Poetry* kept the pace. Viewed in a large perspective, *Poetry* incorporated this immense diversity of talent; and it printed the poets of every range of style and sensibility.

The great variety of poetic achievement which *Poetry* encompassed displays, as we have already noted, the generous catholicity of the editor and the actively radical policies which she introduced. *Poetry*'s radicalism can be best seen by comparing the magazine with others of a similar nature, and the modifications of this radicalism can also be seen by contrasting one issue of *Poetry* with another, a later one. Miss Monroe was radical in the sense that she wanted the poet to return to the fundamental issues of poetry as poetry; and, in order to achieve her purposes, she directed *Poetry* along radical lines. Her radicalism, however, most certainly must not be thought of as a desire for sweeping literary, political, or technological changes. Indeed, Miss Monroe rejected them when they appeared in the 1930's; for she rejected the advanced literary innovations of such writers as James Joyce, Gertrude Stein, and e. e. cummings; moreover, both she and Pound had differed on many occasions over the relative merits of his works. Miss Monroe was never prepared to be either as radical as Pound or as narrow in her likes and dislikes.

In the radical sense, possibly the most immediate thing which *Poetry* hoped to encourage was a greater willingness to experiment and to enforce expanded possibilities for poetic form. Miss Monroe was anxious, as we have noted, that the poet be aware of the present: "Numerous books, and more numerous manuscripts appeal importunately for time and space, whose eager authors seem as unaware of the twentieth-century as if they had spent these recent years in an Elizabethan manor-house or in a vine-clad Victorian cottage."[58] Miss Monroe most strongly objected to the arid, sterile quality of the verse being written at the turn of the century; for this poetry seemed to lack creative originality and imagination—two qualities which the new poetry had in abundance. The poets first had to understand their age and to develop their poetic talent so that they could adequately express that age, not that of bygone years. Miss Monroe's one admonition to the poets was for them to realize the modernity of the age: "The task for the American poet is twice as difficult as it is for his continental brother. The artistic temperament upon which he has to build is solely individual. It is a great tradition, nevertheless, and essentially so in spirit, and it is in the spirit that it must be emulated.[59]

Of the new poetry, Miss Monroe wrote: "The deprecatory, apologetic attitude toward contemporary American art is more to be found in the academic mind trained upon the past and living upon formula." The spirit of tradition was not the target of her attack but the conformity to externals which tradition produced. When the publication of Pound's "Contemporania" in 1913 aroused the vehement criticism that *Poetry* was oblivious to the wisdom of tradition, Miss Monroe was quick to reply: "Their meaning would seem to be tradition of external form rather than the large tradition of spiritual motive, a mere binding tradition of detail for which we confess little reverence. Such tradition is not for the strong, but for the weak."[60] The avowed purpose of *Poetry* was to foster a new spirit of creativity, and this task could not be accomplished if the poets remained dependent upon the worn-out machinery of rhymed eloquence.

In retrospect, the history of modern poetry is definable; for the causes and trends which ultimately shaped the movement come into a clearer perspective. The soundness of certain poetic innovations and experiments in form and style is today accepted because these changes were productive and dynamic. If every change was not intrinsically valuable, the fact that poets were searching for new ways, for new subleties of form and image, had an immense value. The great innovators and masters— Whitman, Pound, Yeats, Eliot, and Auden—made substantial contributions to the main body of modern poetry; and

their achievements became the stimulus for many excellent
minor poets.

When Miss Monroe founded *Poetry*, she had the instinctive
sense that the future greatness of the art must be found in its
engagement with contemporary life and in an expressive lan-
guage as simple and direct as William Wordsworth had de-
manded a century earlier. She constantly urged the poet to
write with greater simplicity of diction and metaphor and to
sever his dependence upon the formal aspects of "rhymed
eloquence." In thus urging the poets to speak in the language
of real men, she was reinforcing the poetic emphasis of the Irish
literary movement. Yeats too had stressed the purer lyricism
of language as a first principle much earlier than the founding
of *Poetry*; and Miss Monroe, in her great respect for Yeats,
recognized in his poetical doctrine the quality of permanent
excellence.

Realizing the value of simplicity of form and diction, Miss
Monroe made these elements key requisites for any poem printed
in the pages of *Poetry*. The magazine always favored simplicity
and sincerity over studied elegance, either of thought or of
style. As late as 1918, Miss Monroe still felt it necessary to
admonish poets: "How often have we urged the poets to forget
the 'magnificent gesture,' and to talk 'in ordinary language of
ordinary things.' "[61] "The new poetry," she wrote, "strives for
a concrete and immediate realization of life. . . . It is less vague,
less verbose, less eloquent, than most poetry of the Victorian
period and much work of earlier periods. It has set before
itself an ideal of absolute simplicity and sincerity—an ideal
which implies an individual, unstereotyped rhythm. It looks
out more eagerly than in; it becomes objective."[62]

VII   *New Poetry and "New Criticism"*

Essentially, Miss Monroe's analysis of the new poetry em-
bodies all of the aspirations for the art that *Poetry* was trying
to realize in its editorial policy. Although Miss Monroe pro-
fessed little sophistication as a critical theorist, she was evalu-
ating the new poetry on the most current principles of modern
criticism. Certainly, her references to T. E. Hulme and his
massive influence are slight; nevertheless, she was attuned to

the dynamics of the critical revolution that was taking place in the first two decades of this century. Ezra Pound was the obvious spokesman for the "new criticism," and Miss Monroe unconsciously accepted many of his ideas on poetry; he gave articulate form to many of the poetic notions that she already possessed. She adopted and amplified the critical concepts that whirled around the formation of Imagism. Her critical contention that the new poetry "looks out more eagerly than in; it becomes objective" supports the view that the best poetry is realized in a dramatization and concrete rendering of form and content. In a less precise way, her notion suggests the more exacting demands of T. S. Eliot's "objective correlative." Her desire that poetry be objective is at least a parallel demand that the poet render his materials poetically with immediacy and fullness.

She was equally indebted to Pound and the "critical revolution" for the rejection of poetry which was essentially personal and subjective. Although the word "objective" is the prevailing critical term, two significantly different notions are implied by it. In the first sense, "objective" possesses the meaning of "realized, or made concrete"; this definition is, of course, Eliot's sense of the term in his exploration of the "objective correlative." The second meaning of the word is its implicit opposition to the "subjective or personal." In the best sense of this traditional meaning, Miss Monroe approved poetry that looked "out more eagerly than in." Poetry of personal emotion or interior anguish was always viewed adversely by the editor and her associates.

Indeed, the poet who depended for his inspiration upon the Romantic notion of himself as a "quivering reed" was rejected. Wherever she detected "personal outpourings" in poetry, she dismissed it as idiosyncratic. Once again, she was operating within the light of the most current critical demands for an *impersonal* poetry. For Miss Monroe, poetry was not a private enterprise; she insisted, as we have observed, that the poet share in the life and culture of the age and that poetry objectively communicate to the mass of men.

Maintaining the view that poetry be objective, it was natural that Miss Monroe—and therefore *Poetry*—was not wholly sympathetic to the subjective poets who came to the fore in the late 1920's and early 1930's. She had a strong prejudice against poetry which was highly introspective, or against poems which required unusual talent or knowledge on the part of the reader. In her mind, lucidity was always a virtue, obscurity, a vice. *Poetry* had been able to sail through its early years because the dominant efforts of the poets had been lyrical, but the poetry of these later decades presented an entirely new problem for the magazine. While modern poetry had successfully created a new precise language for poetic insight, the poets—in Miss Monroe's judgment—soon interjected the destructive element of inversion, an increasing dependence upon private insight and private language. That she felt very keenly about this trend can be seen in her estimate of Ezra Pound's later work:

Of late I have felt that Ezra Pound was sinking too deep in mental easy-chairs of the library, that he was paying the penalty of too much specialization, of isolation with literary groups, apart from the constructive forces which are making the next age. Super-sophistication is more desiccating than ignorance—the artist needs to refresh himself continually at the primal springs of life, by intercourse with simpler people who plant and build and invent, and with powerful people who do these things mightily and direct the energies of the world.[63]

In Miss Monroe's judgment, the future of poetry rested not upon the esoteric but upon the process of direct communication; poetry which failed to have this quality of immediacy made disproportionate demands upon the audience. As early as 1928, she had cause to lament the direction of the current group of poets:

Once more we have "the doctrine of the folding-in, the closure, the esoteric—the aristocratic conception of the Poet, the ancient spirit of caste." The poet aims at being unintelligible to all but the specialists, deliberately discards all the common aids which the ordinary reader is accustomed to, such as punctuation, capitalization, lineation, grammar, syntax, sentence structure, etc., telescoping the English language into hints, exclamations, tip-toeing the high spots of his mood.[64]

Miss Monroe's concept of esoteric poetry extended not only to poetry that was not intelligible without external aid but also to poetry which displayed linguistic idiosyncrasies—or "typographical gymnastics" as she preferred to call them. The chief defects of "these esoteric intellectuals," was, she claimed, that they "were following a tangent from the main curve of the modern movement, a tangent which would inevitably carry them farther and farther into thin-air spaces, remote from both art and life." This special quality of remoteness from life was a most objectionable characteristic in Miss Monroe's mind; to violate the bonds that art has to life was to remove art to a realm of isolation—one without reference to life which was the source of art.

While Miss Monroe felt that the works of such poets as Ezra Pound (especially in the *Cantos*), William Carlos Williams, Hart Crane, Allen Tate, Laura Riding, Yvor Winters, and of others who followed the lead of some of these, were intellectually remote—and both extravagant and artificial—she still printed their work. "*Poetry* has printed many of these poets, but not with the wide-open hospitality which complete sympathy might have demanded."[65] With respect to the so-called esoteric poet, it was more a question of his sincerity which puzzled Miss Monroe. Her own attitudes toward poetic art tended to be far more conservative. "We have endured the reproaches of the extremists," she wrote, "because our ideas of poetic art tend rather toward simplicity, intelligibility, recognizably poetic rhythm."[66] Such poetry, she thought, was extremist and tangential to the fruitful curve of modern poetry, and the editorial policy of *Poetry* was to follow the "grander curve": "I still feel that progress in the art lies along the good curve of solid earth rather than along the euphistic tangent, and that *Poetry* has followed this grander curve."[67]

Miss Monroe never attempted to hide her prejudice against poems which were opaque in thought—or what she termed "cryptic intellectuality which leaps from crag to crag with little consideration for less agile followers." Indeed, if we scan the pages of *Poetry*, few poets of "cryptic intellectuality" are found. Miss Monroe felt that such poems merited only a kind of quiet derision rather than critical approbation. In perhaps her most vehement editorial, she berated the "bulky gods":

Why not laugh at Ezra Pound and all the other exiles and their rages? From over there they laugh at us, and stamp their feet and swear at us, and curse our "mechanized" civilization, and long to come back and set it right. . . . Why not laugh, for example, at

Gertrude Stein, who indeed must long to laugh at herself when
her worshippers gather at her solid knees, and listen solemnly to
the cryptic utterances strung off darkly by her imperious mind. . . .
Why not laugh at that bulky god, James Joyce, when his genius gets
all tangled up in words, when his sentences stretch like lost armies
over pathless pages, with never a comma or a period to light the
wanderer home.[68]

Although she maintained strong attitudes about esoteric
poetry, Miss Monroe was not so narrow or so insular as to
banish the poets who wrote in this vein from the pages of
Poetry. But the magazine undeniably suffered because Miss
Monroe was reluctant to give her aggressive support to many
artists whom she considered "esoteric." According to one former
associate editor, Poetry printed far too many love lyrics from
the pens of middle-aged unmarried ladies during the 1930's.
Apparently, these innocent love lyrics were the only alternatives
to the esoteric and the Marxian poets (the greater of two evils
in Miss Monroe's mind).

In summary, Miss Monroe's taste has been called, as we have
seen, "catholic" by innumerable critics of the magazine; but
the impression of the term does not account for her failure
to discern the modern temper more clearly in the poetry of the
1920's and 1930's. The older values of assurance, optimism, and
progress were absent in the newer poetry; but she was too
imbued with the spirit of confidence from an earlier generation.
Accepted as a term of praise, she was "catholic" in her poetic
judgment in that she tried to balance the demands of many
diverse strains and voices in modern poetry. In this endeavor,
she succeeded in a very large measure. With a tolerant
spirit, she gave the poets a place before the public. The charge
that her taste was not so advanced or so eclectic as it might
have been should not eclipse the more dominant features of
her character; for, as Frederick J. Hoffman has stated, "No one
can question her directness and sincerity, her discriminating
and sensitive taste."[69] Under the hands of a less determined
editor, Poetry might have forged ahead, might have taken many
directions—if Miss Monroe had chosen to espouse a radically
eclectic view. But she was also too farsighted not to realize
that such a view would have led to the death of Poetry. In
her best lights, she chose to keep the magazine free, to maintain

Poetry: A Magazine of Verse   93

an open-door policy, and to print the best poetry as she saw it
shaping itself for its time.

VIII Poetry's Service

"Asked what is at the core or center of *Poetry*'s historical being, one
can perhaps best answer that *Poetry* is, finally, a trade journal."[70]

In Reed Whittemore's recent study of "little magazines," he
has declared that all "little magazines" are incomprehensible
without reference to their real or imaginary responsibilities;
and he has expressed the central ideological issue of the "little-
magazine" world. Because the editors of *Poetry* have been for
the last fifty years "so scrupulous in their efforts to fulfill their
imagined obligations to poets and poetry,"[71] they have been
criticized for evading responsibilities elsewhere. Indeed, Whitte-
more weaves a complex argument to assert that *Poetry*'s evasion
of responsibilities vastly diminished its force as an instrument
for a more vital and intelligent culture.

Because *Poetry* took a craft view and because it failed to
conceive highly enough of poetry, Whittemore asserts that the
influence of the magazine has been forever limited. The late
nineteenth-century concept of the value of poetry (and Matthew
Arnold's well-known proposition is significant here) as an in-
strument that would save civilization was notably absent in
Miss Monroe's own concept of the function of art. For her,
there was no underlying civilization-saving theory, only a rather
"narrow, issue-by-issue preoccupation with printing verse that
is rhetorically clean, descriptively sharp, thematically unplati-
tudinous, and generally 'adequate.' "[72] In essence, what Whitte-
more deplores was *Poetry*'s failure to engage in the political
issues of the culture it served, as well as its narrow concept of
poetry as craft. His argument is made more convincing by con-
trasting *Poetry* with such magazines as *Partisan Review,* the
Fugitive, the *Southern Review,* the *Kenyon Review,* and the
Sewanee Review. Because these magazines engaged the culture,
because they came to grips with issues and were committed,
they influenced and changed that culture significantly. The
difference, Whittemore maintains, is the difference between
estheticism and engagement.

In its earliest days, *Poetry* possessed a crusading spirit, one motivated by the desire to restore poetry as an honored art in the contemporary scene. Few critics have denied the brilliance of *Poetry*'s achievement; indeed, as we have observed, a number of literary historians have dated the beginnings of modern poetry with the founding of Miss Monroe's magazine, a seemingly ample testament of its influence. Today, *Poetry* is still recognized by the aspiring or by the established poet as a place of prestige for displaying new works. The magazine is respected by all who are seriously interested in the art of poetry. This success was prepared for in the first issue of *Poetry* when Miss Monroe declared the purpose of the magazine and frankly recognized that every interest must have its outlet. Her vision of *Poetry* was to provide the poet with a place to display his work, to give the poet the opportunity to communicate with an audience. Indeed, she made the analogy of *Poetry* with the interests of the trade journal in his first editorial, "The Motive of the Magazine."

Whittemore's trenchant criticism is, nevertheless, significant because it touches the heart of *Poetry*'s limitations and because, in substance, many of the critics of the magazine share this view of *Poetry*'s lack of engagement with vital issues. Ezra Pound's great controversy with Miss Monroe grew, as we have seen, out of her refusal to take a more dogmatic stand. Most of *Poetry*'s more unsympathetic critics have charged that the magazine settled for the "adequate" rather than the "excellent" and that Miss Monroe was "conservative" rather than "vitalizing"—that her spirit of adventure was, indeed, timid. In essence, Whittemore claims that Miss Monroe was possessed of no doctrine, "except the platitudinous proposition that literature has important values that should be preserved." To Whittemore, *Poetry* "has in effect made a virtue of compromise, has turned longevity and persistence and representativeness in the publishing of verse into cultural capital."[73]

As a poet and as editor, no one was more sensitive to the conflicting claims of poetry as an art and as a vehicle for ideas. From the esthetic side, the history of *Poetry* proclaims its success. As we have shown, *Poetry*, from its inception to the present, has printed almost every major American and British poet to come to the fore in this century; it has given space to every form of linguistic and formalistic experiment in poetry. Its record of encouragement for innovation has been one of the continuing principles of its editorial policy. But we must admit that the theoretic claims for a "poetry of ideas" fared less spectacularly under the editorship of Miss Monroe. She was not by nature a revolutionary spirit, and poetry which imposed a political idea too forcefully never met her editorial approval.

In the best sense in which Eliot meant the phrase, Miss Monroe too was concerned with "poetry as poetry, and not another thing." She did not move easily between the two worlds of poetry and cultural history. If—as in Whittemore's terms—it seemed "platitudinous" to assert that "literature has important values," Miss Monroe would have gladly accepted the charge. Unlike the more polemic periodicals—such as *Partisan Review*—*Poetry* was guided by design from entering "entangling alliances." If such disengagement seems platitudinous, Miss Monroe was aware of the limited, although intensely valuable, contribution which *Poetry* could and did make.

Poetry has always been true to its "open-door" policy; it has been one of the great testing grounds for new poets; it has listened attentively to the new voices of modern poetry. To maintain otherwise is false and unjust. "Longevity, persistence, and representativeness" are virtues, not defects. *Poetry* continues to exist today—it has continued to serve the poet—because Harriet Monroe had the inherent wisdom not to allow the magazine to become a partisan tool, not to be the voice of the cultural polemic, but to care deeply for the important values of literature. To judge the future possibilities of a poetic talent is surely one of the most hazardous judgments: that Miss Monroe encouraged so many poets whose later work proved permanently interesting must surely be credited to the soundness of her critical insights.

CHAPTER *4*

Harriet Monroe as Poet

I *Early Poetry and Poetic Drama*

AS NOTED earlier, Harriet Monroe's first published poem
appeared in *The Century* in May, 1888. Many years later
she recorded in her autobiography the "exhilaration" of a
first acceptance, an excitement that seemed at that time to
foreshadow in her mind the beginning of a new career. Her
early poetic efforts were admired by such established poets and
critics as Eugene Field and E. C. Stedman; and, to a young
woman, this encouragement fortified her hopes. In the inter-
vening years between the publication of her first poem and
the founding of *Poetry*, Miss Monroe continued to write and
to submit her work to the various journals and magazines of
the time, but the many rejections were disheartening. Her own
disappointing experience with editors as she tried to bring
her poems to print was one of the prime motives which en-
couraged her to establish *Poetry*.

Miss Monroe's career as a poet is one obviously intertwined
with her activities as an editor. The inseparableness of these
two careers and the cross-currents of mutual influences makes
a straightforward analysis of her work as a poet difficult. I do
not wish to recount the various turns which Miss Monroe's career
as a poet took, but I intend rather to restore to print a number
of poems which best reflect her talent. As a younger woman
and before the advent of *Poetry*, she had achieved a very re-
spectable record of publication.[1]

Almost without exception, Miss Monroe's poems may be
labeled "occasional." In the earliest days of her career, she
was very much a product of the "genteel" literary tradition;
and her poems of this period tend, therefore, to be slight in

96

subject matter and to be lyric in tone and form. Her first published poem is a fair example of her poetic capacity at this stage of her career.

With Shelley's Poems

To W.S.M.

Now do I send you to the heights of song,
My brother! Let your eyes awake as clear
As morning dew, within whose crystal sphere
Is mirrored half a world; and listen long,
Till in your ears, famished to keenness, throng
The bugles of the soul—till far and near
Silence grows populous, and wind and mere
Are phantom-choked with voices. Then be strong—
Then halt not till you see the beacons flare
Souls mad for truth have lit from peak to peak;
Haste on to breathe the intoxicating air—
Wine to the brave and poison to the weak—
Far in the blue where angels' feet have trod,
Where earth is one with heaven, and man with God.

1888, *The Century*

Miss Monroe's affection for Shelley pervades the poem and dominates the imagery. The tone is heightened to a kind of strident oratory, supported by an artificial diction. To find such characteristics is not surprising in a youthful poet, but the more abiding fault of a false "poetic" tone was a distinction that was not easily made by her in these early efforts. Miss Monroe was not formally educated in a more diverse literary tradition; hence, she tended to imitate the poetic poses of the most successful men she knew—William Vaughn Moody, Clarence Stedman, Eugene Field, and others.

The marks of the "genteel" tradition are even more apparent in a number of verse dramas which Miss Monroe wrote before the turn of the century. This collection of plays, *The Passing Show,* first published in 1903, included—according to the subtitle—five modern plays in verse. It is pointless to be negatively critical of these plays; they have never been revived, and it is unlikely that they will be. Miss Monroe's work as a dramatist was an interlude in her poetic career, a period in which she attempted to invest her poetry with the concreteness and vivacity of dramatic life. The main point is that the plays reflect her willingness to experiment with forms and voices of poetic expression. Her talent for the art of playwrighting was undoubtedly derivative, and it was basically because of her frustrated efforts to succeed as a poet that she first turned her attention to poetic drama.

The majority of these short plays were done under the tutelage of her many literary friends from The Little Room. During this period, Chicago was trying to establish itself as a theatrical center of the Midwest; and there was considerable activity by local theater managers to secure original scripts from young writers. However, within Miss Monroe's own history as a young writer, the plays have a distinct interest in tracing her development as a poet.

At this stage of her career, she did not possess the powers of architecture so necessary for a sustained, long work; nor had she been able to adapt perfectly the realism of dialogue to the verse form. As a consequence, the plays are defective in structure; and the verse seems more imposed than inevitable. What is important in these plays is the strenuous effort to relate the poetic medium to modern life. Two plays, *It Passes By* and *The Thunderstorm*, are excellent examples of her effort to make poetry relevant to the contemporary scene. Each play treats a modern situation relevant to the life of the audience of the era. And in an age when Shaw and Ibsen were almost unknown in America—in the Midwest at least—Miss Monroe's aspiration to create drama out of contemporary life foreshadowed the same critical notion she later applied to poetry. In spite of the defects of these works—inflated poetic diction, fragmented plot—the plays are variously marked by a rich symbolic element and by a strong insight into the pain of life, two features of her work which had significance for her later poetry.

II *The "Columbian Ode"*

Up to this point, I have bypassed her famous "Columbian Ode" because the poem was itself a unique effort in her career; the circumstances surrounding the composition of this poem have been recounted in Chapter 2. The public occasion of the

poem necessarily dictated the form and tone of celebration,
but the poem is notable for its measured cadence and spirit
of modernity. From the vantage point of its time, 1892, the
great Columbian Exposition was a promise of progress as the
world moved into a new century. The sense of confidence that
surrounded this international event established in many people
a confident attitude toward the ability of man to conquer what-
ever was adverse in nature, and, through his vast ingenuity,
to bring about unprecedented progress. Miss Monroe's "Ode"
expresses this optimism.

Miss Monroe was always justifiably proud of her "Columbian
Ode"; and, through the many years that followed its initial
publication, she frequently recited the poem from memory for
visitors to the office of *Poetry*. For her, one of the special appeals
of the poem was its confidence in the future. This work—perhaps
better than any other of her poems—epitomizes a perspective of
mind that was one of the most stable features of Miss Monroe as
a poet and editor. The following excerpts from the "Columbian
Ode" convey the general spirit of progress that infuses the
whole poem:

> Columbia, on thy brows are dewy flowers
> Plucked from wide prairies and from mighty hills.
> To this proud day have led the steadfast hours;
> Now to thy hope the world its beaker fills.
> The old earth hears a song, sees rainbow gleams,
> And lifts her head from a deep couch of dreams.
> Her queenly nations, elder-born of Time,
>   Troop from high thrones to hear,
> Clasp thy strong hands, tread with thee paths sublime,
>   Lovingly bend the ear.
> Spain, in the broidered robes of chivalry,
> Comes with slow foot and inward-brooding eyes.
> Bow to her banner! 'twas the first to rise
>   Out of the dark for thee.
> And England, royal mother, whose right hand
> Molds nations, whose white feet the ocean tread,
> Lays down her sword on thy beloved strand
>   To bless thy wreathed head;
> Hearing in thine her voice, bidding thy soul
> Fulfill her dream, the foremost at the goal.

And France, who once thy fainting form upbore,
Brings beauty now where strength she brought of yore.
    France the swift-footed, who with thee
    Gazed in the eyes of Liberty,
    And loved the dark no more.

    Around the peopled world
    Bright banners are unfurled;
The long procession winds from shore to shore.
    The Norseman sails
    Through icy gales
To the green Vineland of his long-ago.
Russia rides down from realms of sun and snow,
    Germany casts afar
    Her iron robes of war,
And strikes her harp with thy triumphal song.
Italy opens wide her epic scroll,
In bright hues blazoned, with great deed writ long,
And bids thee win the kingdom of the soul.
And the calm Orient, wise with many days,
From Hoary Palestine to brave Japan
    Salutes thy conquering youth;
Bidding thee hush while all the nations praise,
Know, though the world endure but for a span,
    Deathless is truth.
Now unto these the ever-living Past
Ushers a mighty pageant, bids arise
Dead centuries, freighted with visions vast,
Blowing pale mists into the Future's eyes.
    Their song is all of thee,
    Daughter of mystery.
· ·

    O strange divine surprise!
    Out of the dark man strives to rise,
And struggles inch by inch with toil and tears;
Till suddenly God stoops from his bright spheres,
    And bares the glory of his face.
    Then darkness flees afar,
    This earth becomes a star—
    Man leaps up to the lofty place.
So these who dared to pass beyond the pale,
For a rash dream tempting the shrouded seas,
Sought but Cathay; God bade their faith prevail
To find a world—blessed his purposes!

The hero knew not what a virgin soul
Laughed through glad eyes when at her feet he laid
The gaudy trappings of man's masquerade.
She who had dwelt in forests, heard the roll
Of lakes down-thundering to the sea,
Beheld from gleaming mountain-heights
Two oceans playing with the lights
Of night and morn—ah! what would she
With all the out-worn pageantry
Of purple robes and heavy mace and crown?
    Smiling she casts them down,
      Unfit her young austerity
Of hair unbound and strong limbs bare and brown.

    Yet they who dare arise
    And meet her stainless eyes
Forget old loves, though crowned queens these be.
    And whither her winged feet fare
    They follow though death be there—
So sweet, so fleet, so goddess-pure is she.
Her voice is like deep rivers, as they flow
    Through forests bending low.
Her step is softest moonlight, strong to force
    The ocean to its course.
Gentle her smile, for something in man's face,
World-worn, time-weary, furrowed deep with tears,
Thrills her chaste heart with a more tender grace.
Softly she smooths the wrinkles from his brow
    Lined by the baleful years,
Smiles sunshine on the hoar head, whispers low
New charges from the awakened will of Truth—
Words all of fire, that thrill his soul with youth.
Not with his brother is man's battle here;
The challenge of the earth, that Adam heard,
His love austere breathes in his eager ear.
And so the knight who had warred at his king's command,
And scarred the face of Europe, sheathes his sword,
Hearing from untaught lips a nobler word,
Taking new weapons from an unstained hand.
With axe and oar, with mallet and with spade,
She bids the hero conquer, unafraid
Though cloud-veiled Titans be his lordly foes—
Spirits of earth and air, whose wars brook no repose.
. . . .

Lo, clan on clan,
The embattled nations gather to be one,
Clasp hands as brothers on Columbia's shield,
Upraise her banner to the shining sun.
Along her sacred shore
One heart, one song, one dream—
Men shall be free forevermore,
And love shall be law supreme.

When foolish kings, at odds with swift-paced Time,
Would strike that banner down,
A nobler knight than ever writ or rhyme
Has starred with fame's bright crown
Through armed hosts bore it till it floated high
Beyond the clouds, a light that cannot die!
Ah, hero of our younger race!
Strong builder of a temple new!
Ruler, who sought no lordly place!
Warrior, who sheathed the sword he drew!
Lover of men, who saw afar
A world unmarred by want or war,
Who knew the path, and yet forebore
To tread, till all men should implore;
Who saw the light, and led the way
Where the gray world might greet the day:
Father and leader, prophet sure,
Whose will in vast works shall endure,
How shall we praise him on this day of days,
Great son of fame who has no need of praise?
How shall we praise him? Open wide the doors
Of the fair temple whose broad base he laid.
Through shining halls a shadowy cavalcade
Of heroes moves on unresounding floors—
Men whose brawned arms upraised these columns high,
And reared the towers that vanish in the sky—
The strong who, having wrought, can never die.
. . . .

Strange splendors stream the vaulted aisles along—
To these we loved celestial rapture clings.
And music, borne on rhythm of rising wings,
Floats from the living dead, whose breath is song.

Columbia, my country, dost thou hear?
Ah! dost thou hear the songs unheard of time?

Hark! for their passion trembles at thy ear.
Hush! for thy soul must heed their call sublime.
Across wide seas, unswept by earthly sails,
Those strange sounds draw thee on, for thou shalt be
Leader of nations through the autumnal gales
That wait to mock the strong and wreck the free.
Dearer, more radiant than of yore,
Against the dark I see thee rise;
Thy young smile spurns the guarded shore
And braves the shadowed ominous skies.
And still that conquering smile who see
Pledge love, life, service all to thee.
The years have brought thee robes most fair—
The rich processional years—
And filleted thy shining hair,
And zoned thy waist with jewels rare,
And whispered in thy ears
Strange secrets of God's wondrous ways,
Long hid from human awe and praise.

Although the "Columbian Ode" differs greatly from the central techniques and ideas of Whitman, the same pride and confidence in America is present. Indeed, the echoes of the Whitmanian spirit are not accidental; for Miss Monroe was conscious of Whitman's genius as she modeled her own song to the future of America. Moreover, the Exposition presented ample evidence of man's mechanical genius and of his capacity for international cooperation for an age of progressive advancement in all fields of life and art. If human ingenuity and cooperation could produce such a spectacle of grandeur as the Columbian Exposition, what might man not be capable of in the future century? To these immense possibilities Harriet Monroe addressed her ode. In later years, in spite of World War I and the Depression, she never faltered in her belief that we would one day raise ourselves out of the mire and away from petty contention to complete a world of which the Exposition was only a timid intimation of all that man contained for genuine greatness.

In this poem, she abandoned the traditional machinery of the ode form, with its references to the distant spirits of the muse. The central image of the poem is the daring spirit of Columbus who venturously set forth in search of lands unknown. That spirit of energy and discovery—for the "rash dream tempting the shrouded seas, ... To find a world"—was the force that made man great. The invocations to the ancient muses were no longer appropriate to modern man; and, as the poet cele-brated this new spirit of discovery, she spoke to the spirit of humanity in images of man and his human daring. The language of the poem, which had to be closer to the living spirit of America, is a rhapsodic voice that celebrates man's immensity.

III *Later Poetry*

After the "Columbian Ode," Miss Monroe never again wrote a poem of such sweeping scope. But the discipline imposed by the verse drama of these early years had been helpful in purging her work of the more conventional and self-conscious "poetic diction"; and the drama demanded that the poet ob-jectify emotion—a necessity that gave her later work more explicit firmness.

In 1914, when Harriet Monroe had been the editor of *Poetry*, her second collection of poems, *You and I*, was published. No doubt her position as editor gave her greater critical perspective about her own work; and the poems of this new collection are radically different from some of her earlier ones, such as "Dance of the Seasons" or "Ten Years Old." In contrast to her previous poetry, several important differences emerge; she displayed a considerable advance in technique and greater expertise in handling theme. In addition, we also find an aggressive experi-mentation with new forms and types of poetry. One element which emerges quite clearly is the lesson of Imagism: a greater precision of language and a more accurate focus of image. The subject matter and language are equally radical; but, by the standards of today's poetry, her work may seem unspectacular. The poems are still drawn very directly from her own experi-ence; hence, the mode of these poems is personal and lyrical. In almost all of the poems, she managed to fashion a language far closer to the simplicity of diction which Yeats had so highly recommended; and there is no longer the note of strained diction or any of the artificiality so prevalent in her plays.

The major subdivisions of *You and I* reflect a personalized lyricism as Miss Monroe tried to bring into poetic focus her emotional encounter with nature and other human beings. She divided the poems into two major categories: "Myself" and "Other People." In spite of the seeming personal category, "Myself," the poems are not autobiographical in the strict sense; they are best conceived as human experiences given shape by the voice of the poet. The initial poem of the work, "Myself," displays several interesting aspects of Miss Monroe's poetic orientation.

Myself

What am I? I am Earth the mother,
  With all her nebulous memories;
And the young Day, and Night her brother,
  And every god that was and is.

As Eve I walked in paradise,
  Dreaming of nations, braving death
For knowledge; nor begrudged the price
  When the first baby first drew breath.

I sang Deborah's triumph song;
  I struck the foe with Judith's sword;
'Twas I who to the angel said,
  "Behold the handmaid of the Lord!"

I was fair Helen, she for whom
  A nation was content to die;
And Cleopatra, in whose doom
  The world went down with Antony.

I am the harlot in the street,
  And the veiled nun all undefiled;
In me must queen and beggar meet,
  Wise age hark to the little child.

I am the life that ever is,
  And the new glory that shall be;
The pain that dies, and the brave bliss
  That mounts to immortality.

The capacity for imaginative projection into the historical past indicates a lingering Romantic note in this poem; and, while she did not look to the past with nostalgia, she was nevertheless influenced by the poetic models of much Romantic literature. Indeed, a fascination for the distant and the exotic informs a number of her works, but this interest is also balanced by new influences of sound patterns. Still other poems in the collections display her willingness to experiment in many forms and voices. "The Moment" and "Plaint" are both experiments in sound very much in the vein of Vachel Lindsay. "Plaint" exhibits this consciousness of a heavy metrical pattern.

Plaint

Gaunt Age is stalking me, with Death
Shaking his rattle close behind—
Yet scarcely have I used my breath,
Yet have my eyes been curtained blind.

The world is wide and luminous,
With cities carved in strange designs.
Soon I must sail for Singapore,
On Ankor's towers are mystic lines.
Forests all orchid-hung and dark
The lordly Amazon cuts through;
And far beyond and high above
Rise Inca-temples of Peru.

Alaska slants her shining snows,
And India burns under the sun.
All these my mortal eye would see,
All men alive are calling me;
Yet these were all too lightly won,
For I would go where none has gone
And read the riddle no man knows.

In large measure, *You and I* represents the important preoccupations of Harriet Monroe in those years immediately preceding the founding of *Poetry*. Some of the more notable poems in *You and I* take their theme in the frank acceptance of the machine as one of the glories of man's ingenuity. "The Turbine" and "A Power-Plant" are among the first examples in our literature of an honest celebration of the great potential of mechanical inventiveness brought to ease the burden of life:

The Turbine
To W. S. M.

Look at her—there she sits upon her throne
As ladylike and quiet as a nun!
But if you cross her—whew! her thunderbolts
Will shake the earth! She's proud as any queen,
The beauty—knows her royal business too,
To light the world, and does it night by night
When her gay lord, the sun, gives up his job.
I am her slave; I wake and watch and run
From dark till dawn beside her. All the while
She hums there softly, purring with delight
Because men bring the riches of the earth
To feed her hungry fire. I do her will
And dare not disobey, for her right hand
Is power, her left is terror, and her anger
Is havoc. Look—if I but lay a wire
Across the terminals of yonder switch
She'll burst her windings, rip her casings off,
And shriek till envious Hell shoots up its flames,
Shattering her very throne. And all her people,
The laboring, trampling, dreaming crowds out there—
Fools and the wise who look to her for light—
Will walk in darkness through the liquid night,
Submerged.

      Sometimes I wonder why she stoops
To be my friend—oh yes, who talks to me
And sings away my loneliness; my friend,
Though I am trivial and she sublime.
Hard-hearted?—No, tender and pitiful,
As all the great are. Every arrogant grief
She comforts quietly, and all my joys
Dance to her measures through the tolerant night.
She talks to me, tells me her troubles too,
Just as I tell her mine. Perhaps she feels
An ache deep down—that agonizing stab
Of grit grating her bearings; then her voice
Changes its tune, it wails and calls to me
To soothe her anguish, and I run, her slave,
Probe like a surgeon and relieve the pain.

We have our jokes too, little mockeries
That no one else in all the swarming world

Would see the point of. She will laugh at me
To show her power: maybe her carbon packings
Leak steam, and I run madly back and forth
To keep the infernal fiends from breaking loose—
Suddenly she will throttle them herself
And chuckle softly, far above me there,
At my alarms.

　　　But there are times, you know,
When my turn comes; her slave can be her master,
Conquering her he serves. For she's a woman,
Gets bored there on her throne, tired of herself,
Tingles with power that turns to wantonness.
Suddenly something's wrong—she laughs at me,
Bedevils the frail wires with some mad caress
That thrills blind space, calls down ten thousand lightnings
To shatter her world and set her spirit free.
Then with this puny hand, swift as her threat,
Must I beat back the chaos, hold in leash
Destructive furies, rescue her—even her—
From the fierce rashness of her truant mood,
And make me lord of far and near a moment,
Startling the mystery. Last night I did it—
Alone here with my hand upon her heart
I faced the mounting fiends and whipped them down;
And never a wink from the long file of lamps
Betrayed her to the world.

　　　So there she sits,
Mounted on all the ages, at the peak
Of time. The first man dreamed of light, and dug
The sodden ignorance away, and cursed
The darkness; young primeval races dragged
Foundation stones, and piled into the void
Rage and desire; the Greek mounted and sang
Promethean songs and lit a signal fire;
The Roman bent his iron will to forge
Deep furnaces; slow epochs riveted
With hope the secret chambers: till at last
We, you and I, this living age of ours,
A new-winged Mercury, out of the skies
Filch the wild spirit of light, and chain him there
To do her will forever.

Look, my friend,
Behold a sign! What is this crystal sphere—
This little bulb of glass I lightly lift,
This iridescent bubble a child might blow
Out of its brazen pipe to hold the sun—
What strange toy is it? In my hand it lies
Cold and inert, its puny artery—
That curling cobweb film—ashen and dead.
But see—a twist or two—let it touch
The hem, far trailing, of my lady's robe,
And quick, the burning life-blood of the stars
Leaps to its heart, that glows against the dark,
Kindling the world.

Even so I touch her garment,
Her servant through the quiet night; and thus
I lay my hand upon the Pleiades
And feel their throb of fire. Grandly she gives
To me unworthy; woman inscrutable,
Scatters her splendors through my darkness, leads me
Far out into the workshop of the worlds.
There I can feel those infinite energies
Our little earth just gnaws at through the ether,
And see the light our sunshine hides. Out there
Close to the heart of life I am at peace.

Miss Monroe was always intrigued by man's inventive capacity, by his ability to harness the energies of the universe and to put them in his control and service. To her, the "machine" was not an enemy but a mysterious friend. In an almost novel way, she poeticized the instruments of modern man; they were his wondrous invention, and as such were the fit subjects for the poet. In "The Turbine" she extols the light-giving power of the machine, a power analogous to the sun. With almost metaphysical conceit, she enthrones the turbine as a grand queen who dispenses her favors upon the people. In both "The Telephone" and "A Power-Plant," Miss Monroe sees a similar glory in "the machine" because they make new horizons accessible to man:

The Telephone

Your voice, beloved, on the living wire,
Borne to me by the spirit powerful

Who binds the atoms and leaps out to pull
Great suns together! Ah, what magic lyre,
Strung for God's fingers, sounds to my desire
The little words immortal, wonderful,
That all the separating miles annul
And touch my spirit with your kiss of fire!
What house of dreams do we inhabit—yea,
What brave enchanted palace is our home,
Green-curtained, lit with cresset stars aglow,
If thus it windows gardens far away,
Groves inaccessible whence voices come
That soft in the ear call where we may not go!

Miss Monroe had the fundamental belief that man—through his inventive genius—could build a world of human happiness. To her, the tools of that new world were promises to man's approaching freedom from the more burdensome tasks of existence:

A Power-Plant

The invisible wheels turn softly round and round—
Light is the tread of brazen-footed Power.
Spirits of air, caged in the iron tower,
Sing as they labor with a purring sound.
The abysmal fires, grated and chained and bound,
Burn white and still, in swift obedience cower;
While far and wide the myriad lamps, a-flower,
Glow like star-gardens and the night confound.
This we have done for you, almighty Lord;
Yes, even as they who built at your command
The pillared temple, or in marble made
Your image, or who sang your deathless word.
We take the weapons of your dread right hand,
And wield them in your service unafraid.

Such subjects as telephones, power plants, and turbines did not fit the preconceived public notion of "poetry." Had she preferred to repeat the experiments in the sentimentalism of Eugene Field, she might have succeeded more readily. In addition to her celebration of the machine as an object of poetic attention, Miss Monroe's innovations in free verse and other musical techniques were very much a part of the radical movement underway in Imagist poetry. In such poems as those cited here, she was therefore as much a contributor to the new movement in modern poetry as many other fine modern poets such as Hilda Doolittle, Rupert Brooke, or John Aldington. Throughout the decade which followed the publication of *You and I,* Miss Monroe occasionally printed a number of her own works in the pages of *Poetry.* In 1924, when many of these new works were published as a collection, they revealed a different poetic mood. The title poem of her new book, *The Difference and Other Poems* (1924), was perhaps her most cogent statement of the prevailing sense of dejections and anxiety that pervaded the postwar years. "I fear for the human spirit left alone/ In Vastness," she wrote in her poem, "1923." For her, the optimism of the "Columbian Ode" had failed; and what had once augured to bring mankind closer as nations had been supplanted by a spirit of dejection. This central poem—"The Difference: 1823-1923"—contrasts thematically the vision of young America struggling to create a national heritage and the destructive forces of the 1920's which—to Harriet Monroe at least—seemed to be a denial of the vital forces of progress and national greatness:

> I fear
> Not only because this devilish god-like power
> Of massed and ordered men
> Turns into fury
> Whenever some autocrat—
> Imperial, proletarian—
> Shouts a proud "I!"
> And waves a patterned rag;
> Fury that reddens
> The green earth, flowered with homes,
> And the blue ship-bearing sea,
> Till hundreds of people, thousands,
> An hundred millions maybe,
> Lie ashen and bloodless;
> I fear not only War—
> War may even cease!—
> But Peace.
>
> I fear for the human spirit left alone
> In vastness—

The other poems of this collection are more modest in scope
and more characteristically brief and lyrical. "Improvisations"
and "At the Prado" are carefully wrought moments of descriptive
lyricism. Frequently, the inspiration for these poems grew from
a special place which evoked a mood. Miss Monroe, an inveterate
traveler, tried to capture in poetry the spirit of place; her
sequence of poems "At the Prado" is a strikingly good series
of lyrics on the paintings displayed at this great museum of
art. Harriet Monroe always believed that the poet should have
as much liberty with subjects of his art and the materials of his
craft as the painter enjoys when he does portraits, landscapes,
narrative murals, in oils, watercolors, pastels, drawings—which-
ever medium may seem most expressive. In this series of "art"
poems, she attempted to achieve that kind of artistic liberty.

At the Prado

El Greco

They call you the Greek, Dominico, but Spain caught you.
They call you the Greek, but what Greek ever cast
     purple shadows or lit purple fires!
They call you the Greek, but you suffered
     in your search for God.
Your half-divine Christ bearing his cross
     was but a way-station on the road—
God was always just beyond, out of reach.
God was a dark shade—the inquisition might have been
     his instrument.
God was a star-blue flame—his saints died for him with joy.
And even the little men you painted, Dominico,
The little Count of This and Prince of That,
Even they had felt the fire—
It burned purple behind their eyes.

Dark and bright—O bright and dark, O cruel and tender,
Have you met William Blake in some lonely walk in Paradise?
And have you found God?

Fra Angelico's Annunciation

Little virgin girl, to you the angel is bowing—
Great Gabriel, with gold-enameled wings.

Little girl in blue, dewy like a gentian at sunrise,
To you comes the angel straight from God.
So sweet, so fresh and fair—no wonder!
As clear as a spring under green leaves,
As innocent as a fluffy baby dove two or three days
        from the egg,
As still as deep-sea water—
To you the angel.

Blessed art thou amongst women, little virgin girl.

Rubens

Here you are, grand old sensualist!
And here are the three goddesses
        displaying their charms to Paris.
It was all one to you—goddesses, saints, court ladies—
Your world was all curves of flesh,
        rolling curves repeated like a shell.
Mary Magdalen was almost as good copy as Venus,
Angels might be as voluptuous as nymphs.

It was a rich old gorgeous world you painted—
For kings or prelates, what mattered!—palace or church!
You had a wonderful glorious time!—
And no doubt the ladies loved you.

A number of other poems on travel and place have a Whit-
manesque expression for the glory of the thing celebrated. Such
poems as "The Theatre of Dionysus" and "Under the Moon"
best illustrate Miss Monroe's intent to render a poetic statement
of beauty in the vastness and grandeur of great monuments.
The potential and immensity of man's accomplishments was,
for Harriet Monroe, a profound and poetic part of life; and
she never ceased to make this notion an element of her poetry.
As a deeply felt idea, it was a controlling source of much that
she personally admired and also of what she accepted as an
editor.

The enduring quality of art was a frequent subject for Miss
Monroe. "A Golden Statuette" reveals not only this element but
also another—contemporaneity—in her work:

A Golden Statuette in the Cairo Museum
To J. F.

Young Tut-an-Khamen, poised upon his shallop,
    Has speared a fish.
The goldsmith-sculptor sees the pose and molds it—
    No king could wish
A prettier immortality! Forever
    In delicate grace
He tells of beauty dead yet never dying,
    Winning his race
With haughty Death. Out of the dark tomb chamber
    He seems to sing
Of joy in some predestinate hereafter
    Worthy a king.

Echoes of Keats and Yeats enforce the notion of permanent beauty, and the arrested moment of the king's pose holds him in a graceful activity of joy. The line-length variation and the muted use of rhyme in the alternate short lines lends a feeling of swaying motion to the figure of the king.

A more freely structured poem, "Under the Moon" sets the tone for a number of lyrics that were inspired by scenes of ancient cities or ruins. Different from the Byronic world of faded glory, Miss Monroe's poems express a feeling of awe for the monuments of the past because they are themselves a living link with man's power for beauty.

Under the Moon

By day the Parthenon mourns for its shattered columns,
For its carved gods in exile and its lost Athena,
For all the outrages of defacing Time.
By night it dreams under the silver moon,
Dreams that all is once more perfect as of old.
The scars fade away, the old gods reign again,
The Pan-Athenaic processions move through the sacred
    colonnade
To ghost-music of lyre and tamborine and flute,
And moon-fires are lit on the altar.

Oh beautiful, dream-lovely in the moonlight,
The temple lifts lightly skyward from its wall-bound hill.
The moon blesses it with forgetting and remembering—
The ruin that passes, the glory that endures.

The final line of the poem declares a recognition of the erosion of time, but the enduring "glory" testifies to the greatness of man's aspiration: "The scars fade away, the old gods reign again." Both "Constantinople" and "Jerusalem" are a study in contrast. The faded beauty, "a lady desired and deserted," aptly portrays the agony of Constantinople which dreamed "For a world never won." Miss Monroe renders the pathos inherent in the dreams of the once beautiful and proud city, the rags of its magnificence still visible; but, like the faded lady, it has been deserted by a jealous and faithless people.

Constantinople

City of Constantine, Stamboul of the sultans,
You are like a lady desired and deserted,
Desired of many lovers and deserted of all.
On a worm-eaten throne you sit beside the mirroring water,
The rags of your magnificence around you;
And your lovers, jealous and faithless,
Are aloof and afraid.

O faded fair one, mourning the past,
Silent and patient who were so royal-proud,
Will you ever rise from your ashen seat
And call East and West together,
Between the ribbon straits and the silken seas
Where the fleets of many nations have battled
For a world never won,
A dream that never came true!

Through a more personal vision, "Jerusalem" honors a different struggle. In the poem, the poet has placed herself in the midst of the holy city: "Who am I that I should reflect and reject/ Here where so many pilgrims have accepted all?" Her own sense of religious disbelief is placed in grave doubt by the faith of "So many pilgrims." The enormity of such faith has given the city its strength to rise again: "Stronger than mountains are your foundations,/ O Jerusalem,/ And loftier than stars your towers."

Jerusalem

Who am I, Jerusalem, that I should climb your streets,
Erect on your sharp knee-wounding stones?

Who am I that I should reflect and reject
Here where so many pilgrims have accepted all?
The Holy Sepulchre, the three orifices for the crosses,
The deep-down tomb of Lazarus where he lay three days,
These are morticed to the truth with blood and tears.
Time has seeded your shrines with beauty—they bloom
    like a garden;
The myths grow little flowers of faith.
None can conquer you—not the Egyptian, nor the
    Babylonian, nor the Roman.
They battered down your walls and burnt your towers
Till not one stone was left upon another,
Yet you rose again.
The Philistine took you, the Moslem, the Crusader,
And General Allenby walked in triumph through your
    Jaffa Gate.
Yet here you stand on your hill,
Secure, invincible.

Stronger than mountains are your foundations,
O Jerusalem,
And loftier than stars your towers.

"The Theatre of Dionysus," "Olympia," and "Apollo of Olympia" are also excellent occasional poems inspired by Miss Monroe's many visits to Greece. The music of "Olympia" mirrors the floating song of the poem itself. A measured and carefully wrought hymn, the poem celebrates the natural life of Olympia, its waving grass and birds, its bright sky, and its blooms in flower.

Olympia

Small flowers bloom in the waving grass
And birds are singing in the pine
Where once between tall columns rose
The Zeus whom Phidias made divine.
The thunderbolt was in his hand—
Men dared not look upon his face.
The fluted earth was but his throne,
The bright sky was his dwelling-place.

Now his proud temple strews the ground,
His altars are but broken stones.

> His gold-and-ivory flesh is dust
> Mixed with his violators' bones.—
> Brief is the hour of gods and men—
> Their carved fame falls that was so fair,
> While wilful beauty blooms in flowers
> And floats in song upon the air.

Written in free verse, "The Theatre of Dionysus" and "Apollo of Olympia" possess the sweeping sense of landscape and its power on the viewer.

The Theatre of Dionysus

> Is this the place, are these the stones
> Where Sophocles first saw Œdipus in the flesh,
> The myth whom his word made man?
> Was it here, Medea killed and died,
> With Euripides, a poet, looking on piteously
> From one of these marble stalls?
> Did Æschylus on this stage weave for boys of Athens
> His rhythm-wreaths of verses over-wise
> To be uttered in choral song when Agamemnon
> Found death?
>
> Little yellow and white flowers spring up between the stones,
> Above us the Acropolis is abloom with temples,
> Through violet air the same sun shines.
>
> How can it be that I am here?

The same sense of surprise and awe is woven into "Apollo of Olympia." In this poem, Miss Monroe honors the forceful beauty of the god Apollo. His breathless beauty shatters the lines of the poem and reflects its impact on the poet. The lines are filled with strong alliterative notes, again suggesting the power of Apollo's beauty.

Inspired by her own visits to the great ancient cities, this group of occasional poems partially portrays Miss Monroe's genuine talent for the lyric. Each poem is excellent in its own right, and she gave poetic substance to her work by a careful artistry of craftsmanship. When read as a group, many of the poems are a substantial remembrance of hope and glory that has not been sentimentalized by nostalgia or regret.

IV *Final Poems*

The final volume of Harriet Monroe's poetry was published in 1935. *Chosen Poems* appeared only one year before her death in September, 1936. For some years, she had been conscious of impending death; and, in the early 1930's, she had begun to arrange her affairs by making various property settlements, by willing all of the official documents relating to *Poetry* to the University of Chicago, and by beginning to write her autobiography. In compiling *Chosen Poems,* she wished to leave a poetic record of her best work from the many active years of her life. This volume is, therefore, a collection of new and previously published poems dating back to the 1890's. Over the years Miss Monroe had experimented with many forms and subjects, and she tried to represent this diversity in *Chosen Poems.*

In judging the quality and scope of her poetry, we must inevitably turn to *Chosen Poems* to make a just estimate; for in it the earlier and more imperfect efforts have been purged, and the more solid and technically fine poems are retained. With rare exception, almost all of the poems cited in this chapter are ones which Miss Monroe retained in her final volume. The categories of works in *Chosen Poems* portray the types and variety of subject: Works of Man, Out of Doors, Then and Now, Lyrics, People, Around the Mediterranean, The War, Elegies, and Beyond.

The style of the poetry is always lucid and provocative. In the longer poems there is a steady sense of pace and structure. It simply was not Miss Monroe's "style" to write on an esoteric level or to submerge her meaning in symbolic imagery. One of the tendencies of modern criticism has been its engagement with polemical poetry; consequently, a large share of critical attention has been devoted to poets who present problems of meaning or whose work is conceived of as an element in a larger structure of a philosophical design. Harriet Monroe— and many other minor poets—have been neglected or undervalued because their works do not present interpretative problems.

In this brief discussion with cited selections of Harriet Monroe's poetry, I have tried to present the poems which

typify both her confident vision of life and her manner and
style as poet. As we read the poems, I think her confidence
in man emerges strongly. This view is certainly apparent in
the "Columbian Ode," and it is equally the unstated perspective
of many of the other miscellaneous poems, such as "The Ocean
Liner" or "The Man of Science Speaks." But Harriet Monroe
knew also that man was the heir of pain and disappointment.
She can, in certain moods, portray this side of life, but she
never makes it a dominant theme. Her consciousness of the
drama of life, as man moves between the poles of massive
achievement and of the frailty and disappointment of life, is a
perfectly balanced drama. The images of man, in diverse poems,
project this sanely hopeful vision; and yet she is sensitive to
the paradoxical nature of reality. Such strangely different poems
as "The Turbine," "Pain," and "Chicago 1933" express her per-
ception of the unbalanced claims of beauty and life:

Chicago 1933

Once more through all your open ways—
Through water gates, by land, by air,
Those ancient reckoners of days,
The nations, come to speak you fair.
Down the long avenues of change
The spoil of centuries they bring
Into a palace brave and strange
Where the new era's dreamers sing.
Keen be our ears to hear that song
Through the loud crash of toppling years—
Faint is the sound that will be strong
When the armed world forgets its fears.
Now while the hero-mind of man
Is venturing through the dark unknown,
You light the paces of his plan
Where the towers gather for his throne.
My city, keep the faith you found
When huts rose on the marshy bar!
Lift up your banners from the ground
Whence Lincoln marched, led by his star!
Hear the new song of man's desire
The wireless winds of dream shall bring
When bold Arcturus lights your fire
And the bright towers leap up to sing.

A number of the poems, slighter in scope, are quiet celebrations of small beauties—the "Carolina Woodcuts," for example:

Carolina Woodcuts

The Blue Ridge

Still and calm,
In purple robes of kings,
The low-lying mountains sleep at the edge of the world.
The forests cover them like mantles;
Day and night
Rise and fall over them like the wash of the waves.
Asleep, they reign
Silent, they say all.
Hush me, O slumbering mountains—
Send me dreams.

White

Purple mountains—oh, purple and blue—
Rippling under the sky;
And against them, nearer and brighter,
The many-colored trees,
With tasseled boughs uplifted,
And flowery young leaves.
And before me, trailing down the slope,
The dogwood, like a snow-nymph,
Leads the filmy-robed Spring.

These charming lyrics proclaim nothing momentous, merely the startled moment of beauty captured in nature's abundance. For Miss Monroe, these moments of revealed beauty were the essence of poetry. The grandeur of our universe was for her not only panoramic; it resided equally in the small moments of loveliness—of color, shape, texture. She had a genuine affection for the beauty of nature and landscape, and she wrote many brief descriptive lyrics in this vein. Among the best of these are "Olympia," "Mountain Song," "At the Grand Canyon," and "The Cataracts."

The Cataracts

The Yosemite leaps from the peaks
And plunges down deep into the valley,

Tossing the Spring from his arms
To her couch of flowers.
Tall as El Capitan the mighty,
From earth to heaven he glistens like a god,
And mountain-loads of snow-waters
    foam into clouds for his feet.
In thunderous peal on peal
He shouts to all the choral fountains—
To silver-fingered Nevada the dancer,
To Vernal, her dark-browed lover,
    massive, square-shouldered,
To Illillouette the fairy, tripping in satin slippers
    down over the rocks.
In huge musical volleys he shouts to them,
And they answer in diapasons
    rolling from mountain to mountain,
And in songs feather-soft, that float away
    airily on the wind.
Rushing, yet forever still,
Tiptoeing the tall sequoias,
The cataracts crown the Summer with rainbows
As they lift crystal cups to her beauty
And chant her praise to the sun.

In the last volume, there are other vignettes which record the special aura of place. These poems—such as "Peking," "Constantinople," and others—were her photographs, pictures which she created and to which she could return with the full memory of delight in the initial scene:

Peking

Dreaming under her roofs of gold
The imperial city sleeps in state,
While warrior nations, flags unrolled,
Come marching through her fortress gate.
Beneath her towered wall, one by one,
The slow contemptuous camels tread,
And through it eager engines run
Over the dust of ages dead.
Peking! close bound in triple walls,
Between the old and new she lies;
The yellow dragon guards her halls,
The blare of trumpets fills her skies.

She stirs out of her age-long sleep
By the worn temples chill and still,
Where Sung and Ming and Mongol keep
Their ghostly watch from hill to hill.
Over the graves of dynasties
The winds of dawn blow free and far—
Heralds of hastening centuries,
With banners flown for peace or war.

O brooding East!
O winds of dawn!
From the night-long feast
The kings are gone.
What guests will come
Down the world's highway
At the roll of the drum
For the day?

Miss Monroe was especially adept in writing these short de-
scriptive poems and in endowing them with an evocative imagery.
Many of the poems were, of course, statements of her personal
response to the strangeness and beauty of places. The poems are
still remarkable little statements of the poetry in life.

In viewing the whole spectrum of Miss Monroe's poetry, we
see, in summary, a collection of work marked by an interesting
diversity of subject and theme. Her active engagement as a
poet expanded over a considerable period, a time span of great
change in the world. In her earliest poems, her voice is more
optimistic. As the decades passed, her poetry sounds a more
tempered hope; for she is never defeated. Her vision was not
an essentially philosophical one, and the reader must not expect
more than she proposed to give. The poems are best construed
as small personal records of moments of joy and beauty in life.

In style and tone, all of the poems present an uncomplicated
and lucid statement. To her, any obscurity was a defect in
poetry; indeed, she frequently refused, as we have noted, many
poems submitted to *Poetry* for reasons of vagueness or ob-
scurity. Her poetic language is a simple language, but she was
perhaps never capable of purging her works of certain Romantic
images; in general, however, the figures of speech are drawn
from contemporary life. Perhaps her vision as a poet was limited

HARRIET MONROE

TWAYNE PUBLISHERS, INC.
31 UNION SQUARE WEST   NEW YORK, N. Y. 10003

and her range of human experience too confined for modern
taste; but much of what she produced as a poet still remains as
a quiet testimony to excellence in modern poetry. Her language,
her subjects, and her insights are now part of the integral
pattern of poetry we call "modern."

CHAPTER 5

The Closing Years

I A New Order for Poetry

AS *Poetry* reached into its third decade, the growing sense of unease and discontentment of the poets was also becoming the dominant characteristic of American letters. The economic disorder of America after 1929 was an international signal for political reorganization; and many of the new poets sought to engage the voice of poetry in the political arena. The early work of Auden and Spender in England and the more minor writings of the Objectivists in America, such as Kenneth Fearing and John Peale Bishop, were filled with the strident sounds of a new political order. As these new poets came to the fore, their work was, as has been observed, unacceptable to Miss Monroe. She refused to believe that they were the representatives of the aspiration and culture of America; for, like the early work of Eliot, the new poets of the 1930's were to Miss Monroe destructive forces. Not only were their philosophical and political assumptions antithetical to her, but the intensified experimentation of their work was almost antiliterary. The grace of music and of the more lyrical emotion was absent from their writings.

For Miss Monroe, the new temper of political unrest was genuinely shocking; and, for a woman of sensibility and breadth of experience, she was surprisingly out of tune with the larger political implications of world events in the early 1930's. Her monthly editorials in *Poetry* during this period of national strife are singularly apolitical. Needless to say, the consequences of this apolitical stance are reflected in the pages of *Poetry* with relatively few exceptions. For the most part, Miss Monroe declined to print the more vigorous pronouncements of the

124

politically oriented poets; but she did continue her practice of permitting special issues of *Poetry* for the publication of poems which were out of sympathy with her views of what the art of poetry was. As the decade progressed, her lack of appreciation or of sympathy with this new poetry became more and more acute as *Poetry* failed to publish the more politically oriented new poets.

The fact that so tenuous an organ as *Poetry* managed to survive through the crucial years of poverty that followed the Depression is itself a testament to Miss Monroe's perseverance. Then in her seventies, she recognized that her editorship was drawing to a close; and she began characteristically to make plans for a new editor to assume the burden and responsibility which she had held for almost thirty years. She was keenly aware that she was becoming increasingly out of touch with some of the more radical poetic experiments of the poets; and she also recognized that the magazine could not prosper intellectually if it had to depend upon a steady diet of innocuous lyrics—poems which were competent but not vigorous.

Recognizing that *Poetry* had lost some of its quality of adventure, Miss Monroe began her quiet search for a successor in the early 1930's; but there seemed ample time to find the right person for the editorship. It was a difficult decision, and many poets for whom she had artistic respect might have easily qualified. Her strongest desire, of course, was for a person whom she could trust to place the life of the magazine above partisan issue. In an effort to gain some perspective on the problem, she sought the advice of a number of the associates and poets. In response to one of her inquiries about Marianne Moore, Pound wrote that she might be an apt choice from Miss Monroe's point of view; but Miss Moore, Pound contended, would be inevitably wrong—for all of the reasons that Pound considered Miss Monroe wrong—because she would not support a really radical poetry.

Needless to say, Miss Monroe temporized since she was not ready to give up the editorship, but her search was instructive; she knew that she could not leave the situation to time and chance. And she clearly did not want the power to fall into the hands of someone who would ultimately destroy *Poetry*—the magazine simply could not become the private instrument

for an esoteric poetry or for a poetry in service of a political
point of view. As events actually shaped themselves, Miss Monroe
never made a final choice for a successor; and, upon her sudden
death in 1936, the editorship was assumed by Morton Dauwen
Zabel, then one of Miss Monroe's most trusted associate editors.

II Poetry *Today*

Today, the most significant visible monument to Harriet
Monroe is the continuous life and vigor of *Poetry,* now in its
seventh decade of existence. As a voice of excellence, *Poetry*
is a part of the permanent history of American letters; and
it is and will continue to be a vital part of the literature of
the future. While Miss Monroe lived, *Poetry* was the devotion
and center of her concern, a genuine sense of responsibility
toward the art she loved from her early girlhood days. Since
her death in 1936, the history of the magazine has been a re-
affirmation of the sound principles which guided its establish-
ment sixty years ago. Morton Dauwen Zabel, who assumed
the editorship upon Miss Monroe's death, has most forcefully
stated the power of the magazine's founder-editor and the power
for greatness which *Poetry* possessed: "What *Poetry* the magazine
derived from the poet who founded it was courage, the eager-
ness for discovery, and the superiority to personal and partisan
demands that have been its certain claim to her own long life
and certainty of motive. . . .*Poetry* has never been surer of its
purposes than when it published manuscripts greeted by im-
mediate contempt, but eventually by recognition, enthusiasm,
and even by the public's complacent satisfaction that in our
age classics may still be added to literature." Gautier's poem,
L'Art, expresses the conviction that "the sovereign song" remains
as a permanent element in the ever changing future.

> —All things return to dust
> Save beauties fashioned well;
> The bust
> Outlasts the citadel.
>
> Oft doth the plowman's heel,
> Breaking an ancient clod,
> Reveal
> A Caesar or a god.

> The gods, too, die, alas!
> But deathless and more strong
> Than brass
> Remains the sovereign song.

III   *The Autobiography*

Conscious that her work was drawing near its end, Miss Monroe had begun her autobiography, *A Poet's Life*, in 1932; and in it she hoped to record her own contribution and that of *Poetry* in the shaping of modern poetry. From the vantage point of 1932, the need to settle the literary history of American poetry must have seemed more urgent. In the decades since Miss Monroe's death, many scholars and analysts have covered the same ground with great thoroughness and detail; but Miss Monroe's autobiography remains a personal and singular document portraying the energy of the struggle to reshape a literary form. Later critics have superseded her in interpreting the larger influences on modern poetry, but what is missing from their accounts is the unique effort of *Poetry* and its personal history.

When Miss Monroe began her work on this personal history, she had at her command a vast fund of personal and public experiences in the literary world dating back to the 1880's. She had been both a knowledgeable figure and a confidante in literary circles that had been major forces in modern poetry. In addition to her intimacy with literary figures, she possessed a fantastic fund of heretofore unpublished letters from many world-renowned poets, letters which were highly revealing of the tension of the creative process in modern poetry. Moreover, her role as editor of *Poetry* for over thirty years made it almost mandatory that she leave a record of her accomplishments. Her autobiography, therefore, is an account of the official formation of *Poetry* and of its trials and triumphs, failures and more remarkable successes, as poetry advanced through the early decades of this century. Of equal importance, however, is the personal element of her book. Without undue pride, she wished to set forth the role which she had played and to have her autobiography be the story of her own creative achievements as a poet and editor.

Without the autobiography, the history of *Poetry*'s finest

achievements would be more enigmatical—it would be more difficult to discern conscious evaluations of merit. The history of any magazine is inevitably the story of the commanding force behind its achievement; and, for *Poetry,* Harriet Monroe was that commanding force. The impress of her personality, the vitality and diversity of her interests, and the native energy which she lent to *Poetry* made it a magazine of distinguished taste and extraordinary stability.

Miss Monroe's autobiography, *A Poet's Life,* is a document, therefore, in the cultural history of American letters, and it is a valuable source book for any study of the Chicago renaissance. As a central figure in the vital movement, Harriet Monroe was a sharp observer—and frequently a chief source of encouragement—of the many talented young writers working in the Midwest. The magnitude and contribution of the Chicago renaissance to our national literature is today well recognized, and the unique addition of Miss Monroe's autobiography completes the record of the personalities and supplies the colorful detail that surrounded this important literary movement. Like the famous Sitwell autobiographies, Miss Monroe's work provides a series of insights into the cultural pattern which produced a significant segment of our national literature. Intrinsically a part of the Chicago renaissance, Harriet Monroe's own life story is most remarkable because her activities and efforts as a poet and editor are central to the larger history of the movement. In writing the autobiography, it was not her plan to be a comprehensive commentator: she wished simply to leave a record of her own life.

In the few remaining years of her life much of Miss Monroe's energies were devoted to the task of the autobiography, *A Poet's Life.* When her activities were not consumed with it or the editing of *Poetry,* she worked intermittently on the editing of *Chosen Poems. A Poet's Life* was nearly finished in 1936 when Harriet Monroe accepted an invitation to be an American representative at the P.E.N. Conference to be held later that year in Buenos Aires. At first, she was doubtful about so distant a journey; and she feared that it might be too great a strain on her already frail physical resources; but, encouraged by her friends and her own love of travel, she began to make plans for the long trip. She left Chicago on August 10, 1936—on what

proved to be her last journey. On September 26, her friends at
Poetry received a cablegram that Miss Monroe had died at
Arequipa, Peru, on her homeward-bound journey.

Of her autobiography she had only a few chapters to com-
plete, and they were to be a record of her experiences and
travels from 1922 to 1936. She had planned to complete the
remainder of the work after her return from the P.E.N. Con-
ference in October. But, meanwhile, she had prepared to write
the final chapter for her book—"a summary of her career and
a statement of her personal beliefs and ideals. That chapter,
begun in Chicago, was taken with her and written out in full
as her steamer carried her from New York to Buenos Aires."[1]
The final chapter of her autobiography was printed as it was
found in her baggage when it was sent back to Chicago after
her death.

Miss Monroe's "final chapter" is a magnificent testament to
the exaltation of life and to the power for beauty which men
possess. It is also a most intimate chapter—a final statement
about the meaning and value of life viewed from the perspective
of one whose life had been very full indeed. With great nostalgia,
she reviewed those singular moments in life when—as she ex-
pressed it—"Beauty becomes sublimity." "At such times the
beauty of life seems too keen to be borne; there are seasons of
joy and sorrow when the chaos of people and purposes assumes
processional dignity, and the babel of tongues becomes a choral
song. It is as if one watched this earthly episode from some far
planet of larger spaces and years, and saw its crisscross of lines,
its blots and splashes of color, merge into a noble pattern set
for the delight of gods." For Miss Monroe to be a part of the
colossal movement of life was a "destiny so sublime as to be
beyond the reach of deliberate thought."[2] The adventure of life
was always filled with hope—the hope that man would one day
realize the greatness of his potential for peace and beauty. To
that end, she had devoted the energies of a lifetime.

The news of her death was received with shock and sorrow
by Harriet Monroe's associates on the staff of *Poetry*. Indeed,
her passing was noted in the press of all the principal cities
of America. The mark which she had left on modern poetry
was richly expressed by Ezra Pound in the December, 1936,
memorial issue of *Poetry*. He wrote: "During the twenty-four

years of her editorship perhaps three periodicals made a brilliant record, perhaps five periodicals, but they were all under the sod in the autumn of 1936, and no other publication has existed in America where any writer of poetry could more honorably place his writings. This was true in 1912. It is true as I write this."

Nothing is more difficult to predict than the future of poetry. In an age when most people would have felt that the time for new action had passed, Harriet Monroe took upon herself the arduous and uncertain task of "predicting the future of poetry."

IV *Conclusion*: *A Contribution to American Literature*

Harriet Monroe was, first, a poet and, second, an editor of uncommon sensibility. She would like, we feel sure, to be remembered for her achievements in that order. History has, however, honored her more dynamic and tangible role of editor. As the founder of *Poetry*, she infused a new vitality into the American poet; she encouraged a new seriousness and a new confidence in the art. Most significantly, she gave the poet a voice, a place from which he could speak with dignity. For Miss Monroe, poetry was not a "cloistered virtue" to be kept pure from the ravisher of time and men. If poetry was ever to achieve a new vitality, believed Miss Monroe, it had to distill that energy from contention and struggle; it had to be a statement of man's responses to human experience. Throughout the decades of her editorship, she fostered this new adventure in poetic statement; therefore, her place as a shaping force in the making of modern poetry is secure. For a young poet today to be admitted to the pages of *Poetry* is a moment of special achievement because he knows he now stands amid a long tradition of excellence; he is absorbed into and becomes a part of the grandeur-shaping movement of American literature.

Miss Monroe's success as an editor has been ascribed to a number of personal and ideological attitudes. There is no doubt that the continued success of *Poetry* derived much from the firmness and stability of its editor, but such characteristics only account for the superficial motives. Her deepest source of insight was her own poetic sensitivity. From her youthful days, she cared for poetry—for its special magic in words and for its unique satisfactions of mind. To be an active poet was the deepest and most abiding commitment of Miss Monroe's life. Because she was a poet first, she was a sensitive critic of poetry.

As a poet, there is a marked development in her work—a movement from the derivative to a mature and characteristic voice. The early poetry and her foray into poetic drama are less distinguished because they represent a young poet's search for her proper medium. The interesting quality of these poems and plays is the note of experimentation, a willingness to launch out in untried directions. This is especially true of her efforts in drama. The plays are inevitably bounded by the limitations of the American theater in the 1890's; but, within that framework, Miss Monroe tried to insert some realism of subject matter, to make the plays deal with the real problems of men and women and not some artificially conceived remote and romantic characters. Her efforts are minor when pitted against those of Ibsen and Shaw; but she was, nevertheless, aware of the rising tide of Realism in drama. Her plays were written in a highly transitional moment in American drama, which only reluctantly shed the trappings of a heroic "poetic drama" for the later Realism of the twentieth century. If Miss Monroe's plays are not fully achieved works, it is because they are a part of national drama in a state of change—written too early for their Realistic content and too late for the waning vogue of high "poetic" drama.

A similar judgment may be conferred upon her early poetry. Too many of the poems are caught up in the tangle of the "romantic diction" of the "genteel" tradition. After the success of her "Columbian Ode" (1892), Miss Monroe struck a more contemporary tone in her work—both in diction and in subject matter. Most of the poetry reprinted in this study was composed after the founding of *Poetry*; it reflects her work after she had been freed of satisfying the demands of commercial publishers. The diction is no longer false, and the themes are no longer tailored to any noble preconception of what poetry should be and do.

Almost all of Miss Monroe's poetry is occasional, prompted by some public or private event. The individual lyrics are marked by a fine perception and technical sophistication; the more descriptive poems—especially those of individual cities—are evocative of the unique historical spirit of place. In judging the quality of her poems, we must recognize that, if her range is personal and limited, the works still have the solidarity and excellence of a good minor poet. She was consistently innovative in her poetic technique, and she sought constantly to make a meaningful statement of life. She had little tolerance for intellectual indirection or for a negative view of life. As a poet, she consciously sought new avenues of expression, and she encouraged the same adventurous spirit in other young poets. Her poetry is a minor contribution to the revolutionary spirit of twentieth-century literature. As for *Poetry*, it, to cite Vernon Watkins, "was the first mouthpiece of poems which have turned the course of our literature!"

Notes and References

Chapter One

1. Frederick J. Hoffman, *The Little Magazine* (Princeton, 1946), p. 39.
2. Harriet Monroe, *A Poet's Life: Seventy Years in a Changing World* (New York, 1938), p. 34.
3. *Ibid.*, pp. 447, 458.
4. Horace Gregory and Marya Zaturenska, *A History of American Poetry: 1900-1940* (New York, 1942), p. 144.
5. Unpublished letter of Harriet Monroe, dated April 24, 1911.
6. Undated letter from William Archer to Miss Monroe and cited in her autobiography, *A Poet's Life*, p. 178.
7. *A Poet's Life*, p. 242.

Chapter Two

1. Gregory, *A History of American Poetry*, p. 11.
2. A. S. Collins, *English Literature of the Twentieth Century* (London, 1960), p. 22.
3. Bernard Duffey, *The Chicago Renaissance in American Letters: A Critical History* (East Lansing, 1956), p. 55.
4. *Ibid.*, p. 57.
5. Monroe, *A Poet's Life*, p. 244.
6. Harry Hansen, *Midwest Portraits: A Book of Memories and Friendships* (New York, c. 1932), p. 258.
7. Monroe, *A Poet's Life*, p. 250.
8. *Ibid.*
9. *The Letters of Ezra Pound: 1907-1941*, edited by D. D. Paige (New York, 1950), p. 9.
10. John Gould Fletcher, *Life Is My Song* (New York, 1937), p. 194.
11. Eunice Tietjens, *The World at My Shoulder* (New York, 1938), p. 24.

Chapter Three

1. Bernard Duffey, *The Chicago Renaissance*, p. 186.
2. Hoffman, *The Little Magazine*, p. 3.

133

3. *A Poet's Life*, p. 289.

4. Stanley K. Coffman, *Imagism: A Chapter for the History of Modern Poetry* (Norman, 1951), p. 47.

5. *Ibid.*, p. 18.

6. *Ibid.*, p. 12.

7. *Ibid.*, pp. 34-35.

8. Unpublished letter of Alice Corbin Henderson, dated June 7, 1916.

9. An editorial comment by Conrad Aiken, quoted by Miss Monroe in *A Poet's Life*, p. 309.

10. *Ibid.*, p. 339.

11. *Ibid.*, p. 341.

12. Harriet Monroe, Introduction, *The New Poetry*, new and enlarged edition (New York, 1923), p. xxxv.

13. *Ibid.*, p. xxxvi.

14. Hoffman, *The Little Magazine*, pp. 4-5 and 32.

15. Unpublished letter of Ezra Pound, dated January 27, 1913.

16. *The Letters of Ezra Pound*, dated August 18, 1912, p. 9.

17. *Ibid.*, p. 35.

18. *Ibid.*, p. 30.

19. *Ibid.*

20. *Ibid.*, p. 41.

21. *Ibid.*, p. 50.

22. *Ibid.*, p. 26.

23. K. L. Goodwin, *The Influence of Ezra Pound* (New York, 1966), p. 14.

24. *Ibid.*, p. 16.

25. *Ibid.*

26. Duffey, *The Chicago Renaissance*, p. 193.

27. Horace Gregory, "The Unheard of Adventure," *The American Scholar*, VI (Spring, 1937), 198.

28. *Ibid.*

29. Ezra Pound, "Vale," *Poetry*, XLIX (December, 1936), 137.

30. *The Letters of Ezra Pound*, dated November 15, 1926, p. 203.

31. Ezra Pound, "Vale," *Poetry*, XLIX (December, 1936), 137.

32. Harriet Monroe, "The Open Door," *Poetry*, I (November, 1912), 64.

33. Harriet Monroe, "The New Beauty," *Poetry*, II (April, 1913), 24.

34. Harriet Monroe, "The Audience," *Poetry*, V (October, 1914), 31.

35. Comment of Jessica Nelson North in a personal interview.

36. Harriet Monroe, "Our Birthday," *Poetry*, VII (October, 1915), 31.

37. Ezra Pound, "Give Him Room," *Poetry*, VI (May, 1915), 83.
38. Hoffman, *The Little Magazine*, p. 18.
39. See Harriet Monroe and Alice Corbin Henderson, eds., *The New Poetry* (New York, 1917), p. xii. This anthology underwent two major revisions during the lifetime of Miss Monroe, and the work has been reprinted fourteen times, the last in 1944.
40. See William Rice, "Ezra Pound and Poetry," *The Dial*, LIV (May, 1913), 371.
41. Morton Dauwen Zabel, "Harriet Monroe," *Poetry*, XLIX (December, 1936), 162.
42. Harriet Monroe, "A Century in Illinois," *Poetry*, XIII (November, 1918), 92.
43. Monroe, *A Poet's Life*, p. 252.
44. *Ibid.*
45. *Ibid.*
46. Harriet Monroe, "The Procession Moves," *Poetry*, XXX (August, 1927), 270.
47. *The Letters of Ezra Pound*, dated October 22, 1912, p. 12.
48. Hoffman, *The Little Magazine*, p. 20.
49. Letter from Jessica Nelson North to the author, dated February 15, 1953.
50. Harriet Monroe, "Looking Backward," *Poetry*, XXXIII (October, 1928), 35-36.
51. Comment of Jessica Nelson North in a personal interview.
52. Gregory, *A History of American Poetry*, pp. 146-47.
53. Harriet Monroe, "Wanted—A Theme," *Poetry*, XXXI (November, 1927), 89.
54. Harriet Monroe, "The Motive of the Magazine," *Poetry*, I October, 1912), 28.
55. Jessica Nelson North, "Convention and Revolt," *Poetry*, XXXIV (July, 1929), 214.
56. Gregory, *A History of American Poetry*, p. 146.
57. The author is indebted to Jessica Nelson North for these rules. As a former first reader, she related the rules from memory; they are therefore not complete, but serve to show the major prejudices of *Poetry*.
58. Harriet Monroe, "The New Beauty," *Poetry*, II (April, 1913), 22.
59. Harriet Monroe, "Tradition," *Poetry*, II (May, 1913), 67.
60. Harriet Monroe, "Colonialism Again," *Poetry*, X (May, 1917), 94.
61. Harriet Monroe, "Back to China," *Poetry*, XI (February, 1918), 272.
62. Monroe, *The New Poetry*, p. vi.

63. Harriet Monroe, "Ezra Pound," *Poetry*, XXVI (May, 1925), 96. This quotation also reveals the sources of Miss Monroe's admiration for the work of such men as Carl Sandburg and Edgar Lee Masters.

64. Harriet Monroe, "Looking Backward," *Poetry*, XXXIII (October, 1928), 35.

65. *Ibid.*, p. 36.

66. *Ibid.*

67. *Ibid.*

68. Harriet Monroe, "Poetry of the Left," *Poetry*, XLVIII (July, 1936), 216.

69. Hoffman, *The Little Magazine*, p. 38.

70. Reed Whittemore, *Little Magazines* (Minneapolis, 1963), p. 16.

71. *Ibid.*

72. *Ibid.*, p. 14.

73. *Ibid.*, pp. 13-16.

Chapter Four

1. See Selected Bibliography for a record of her works to 1912.

Chapter Five

1. Morton Dauwen Zabel in *A Poet's Life*, p. 428. Since Miss Monroe's autobiography was incomplete at the time of her death, Morton Dauwen Zabel, then acting editor of *Poetry*, organized the final version of the book for publication. He wrote Chapters 34 and 36, thus completing the personal and literary record of Miss Monroe's life and achievement. Chapter 35, "Last Words: Past and Future," was discovered in her baggage when it was later returned to Chicago from South America.

2. Monroe, *A Poet's Life*, p. 458.

Selected Bibliography

PRIMARY SOURCES

A. *Works of Harriet Monroe*

1. Books

Valeria and Other Poems. Chicago: De Vinne Press, 1891.
The Columbian Ode. Designs by Will H. Bradley. Chicago: W. I. May and Company, 1893.
John Wellborn Root: A Study of His Life and Work. Boston: Houghton Mifflin Company, 1896.
The Passing Show: Five Modern Plays in Verse. Boston: Houghton Mifflin Company, 1903.
The Dance of Seasons. Designs by Will H. Bradley. Chicago: Ralph Fletcher Seymour Company, 1911.
You and I. New York: The Macmillan Company, 1914.
The New Poetry: An Anthology. Harriet Monroe and Alice Corbin Henderson, editors. New York: The Macmillan Company, 1917.
The New Poetry: An Anthology. Harriet Monroe and Alice Corbin Henderson, editors. Second edition. New York: The Macmillan Company, 1923.
The New Poetry: An Anthology. Harriet Monroe and Alice Corbin Henderson, editors. Revised edition. New York: The Macmillan Company, 1932.
The Difference and Other Poems. Chicago: Covici-McGee Company, 1924.
Poets and Their Art. New York: The Macmillan Company, 1926.
Poets and Their Art. Second edition. New York: The Macmillan Company, 1932.
Chosen Poems: A Selection from My Books of Verse. New York: The Macmillan Company, 1935.
A Poet's Life: Seventy Years in a Changing World. New York: The Macmillan Company, 1938.

2. Articles

"The Motive of the Magazine," *Poetry*, I (October, 1912), 26-28.
"The New Beauty," *Poetry*, II (April, 1913), 22-25.
"Tradition," *Poetry*, II (May, 1913), 67-70.

137

"Poetry A Zest for Life," *Poetry*, II (July, 1913), 140-42.
"Sobriety and Earnestness," *Poetry*, III (January, 1914), 141-44.
"Poetry's Banquet," *Poetry*, III (April, 1914), 25-28.
"The Enemies We Have Made," *Poetry*, IV (May, 1914), 61-64.
"The Poet's Bread and Butter," *Poetry*, IV (August, 1914), 195-98.
"The Audience, II," *Poetry*, V (October, 1914), 31-32.
"Give Him Room," *Poetry*, VI (May, 1915), 81-84.
"Our Birthday," *Poetry*, VII (October, 1915), 30-31.
"The Question of Prizes," *Poetry*, VII (February, 1916), 246-49.
"Down East," *Poetry*, VIII (May, 1916), 85-89.
"Various Views," *Poetry*, VIII (June, 1916), 140-44.
"How Not to Do It," *Poetry*, VIII (July, 1916), 195-97.
"New Banners," *Poetry*, VIII (August, 1916), 251-53.
"The Future of the Magazine," *Poetry*, IX (October, 1916), 33-35.
"Then and Now," *Poetry*, IX (December, 1916), 141-44.
"The New Era," *Poetry*, IX (January, 1917), 195-97.
"Colonialism Again," *Poetry*, X (May, 1917), 95-97.
"Fire of Youth," *Poetry*, X (June, 1917), 154.
"Will Art Happen," *Poetry*, X (July, 1917), 203-5.
"These Five Years," *Poetry*, XI (October, 1917), 33-41.
"A Word to the Carping Critic," *Poetry*, XI (November, 1917), 89-92.
"Back to China," *Poetry*, XI (February, 1918), 271-74.
"The New Internationalism," *Poetry*, XII (June, 1918), 146-49.
"The Great Renewal," *Poetry*, XII (September, 1918), 320-25.
"Aesthetic and Social Criticism," *Poetry*, XIII (October, 1918), 37-41.
"A Radical-Conservative," *Poetry*, XIII (March, 1919), 322-26.
"Editorial Amenities," *Poetry*, XIV (August, 1919), 262-66.
"Back to Nature," *Poetry*, XIV (September, 1919), 328-30.
"What Next?," *Poetry*, XV (October, 1919), 33-38.
"Those We Refuse," *Poetry*, XV (March, 1920), 321-25.
"Discovered in Paris," *Poetry*, XVI (June, 1920), 148-51.
"Their Wide Range," *Poetry*, XVII (March, 1921), 322-25.
"Drinkwater on Abercrombie," *Poetry*, XVIII (April, 1921), 30-35.
"Here in Cass Street," *Poetry*, XVIII (July, 1921), 208-13.
"Poetry and the Allied Arts," *Poetry*, XIX (October, 1921), 31-37.
"Renewal of Youth," *Poetry*, XIX (December, 1921), 146-48.
"The Utterance of Poetry," *Poetry*, XIX (February, 1922), 266-72.
"Newspaper Verse," *Poetry*, XIX (March, 1922), 324-30.
"Prosody," *Poetry*, XX (June, 1922), 148-52.
"Nature the Source," *Poetry*, XX (August, 1922), 266-68.
"Mea Culpa," *Poetry*, XX (September, 1922), 323-27.
"Ten Years Old," *Poetry*, XXI (October, 1922), 32-37.
"Flamboyance," *Poetry*, XXI (November, 1922), 89-90.
"Poets the Self-Revealers," *Poetry*, XXIII (January, 1924), 206-10.

"Sara Teasdale," *Poetry,* XXV (February, 1925), 262-68.
"Illuminations," *Poetry,* XXVI (April, 1925), 36-38.
"Ezra Pound," *Poetry,* XXVI (May, 1925), 90-97.
"Another Birthday," *Poetry,* XXVII (October, 1925), 32-36.
"The Impossible," *Poetry,* XXVII (March, 1926), 324-27.
'Mr. Turbyfill's Poem," *Poetry,* XXVIII (May, 1926), 92-95.
"The Procession Moves," *Poetry,* XXX (August, 1927), 270-73.
"Fifteen Years," *Poetry,* XXXI (October, 1927), 32-37.
"Wanted—A Theme," *Poetry,* XXXI (November, 1927), 86-91.
"The 'Voices' and the 'Singer,'" *Poetry,* XXXII (September, 1928), 330-34.
"Looking Backward," *Poetry,* XXXIII (October, 1928), 32-38.
"Office Amenities," *Poetry,* XXXIII (October, 1928), 38-41.
"Why Not Laugh?," *Poetry,* XXXIII (January, 1929), 206-9.
"A Censorship for Critics," *Poetry,* XXXIV (April, 1929), 32-36.
"Convention and Revolt," *Poetry,* XXXIV (July, 1929), 212-16.
"Quality in Madness," *Poetry,* XXXIV (August, 1929), 270-72.
"Subsidies and Prizes," *Poetry,* XXXV (November, 1929), 92-95.
"They Come and They Go," *Poetry,* XXXVI (September, 1930), 326-30.
"Coming of Age," *Poetry,* XXXVII (October, 1930), 34-37.
"Should He Be Educated?," *Poetry,* XXXVII (November, 1930), 90-95.
"The Arrogance of Youth," *Poetry,* XXXVII (March, 1931), 328-33.
"Leadership," *Poetry,* XXXVIII (May, 1931), 92-95.
"Birthday Reflections," *Poetry,* XXXIX (October, 1931), 32-36.
"Volume Forty," *Poetry,* XL (April, 1932), 30-34.
"Another Chance," *Poetry,* XL (August, 1932), 270-72.
"The Great Poem," *Poetry,* XLI (November, 1932), 90-94.
"A Bull in the China Shop," *Poetry,* XLII (July, 1933), 212-16.
"Twenty-One," *Poetry,* XLIII (October, 1933), 32-37.
"Art and Propaganda," *Poetry,* XLIV (July, 1934), 210-15.
"This Changing World," *Poetry,* XLIV (September, 1934), 330-34.
"Another Birthday," *Poetry,* XLV (October, 1934), 32-40.
"A. E.," *Poetry,* XLVI (September, 1935), 334-36.
"Poetry's Old Letters," *Poetry,* XLVII (October, 1935), 30-39.
"Joy in Great Art," *Poetry,* XLVII (January, 1936), 208-12.
"Present-Day Tendencies," *Poetry,* XLVIII (June, 1936), 152-57.
"Poetry of the Left," *Poetry,* XLVIII (July, 1936), 212-21.
"Poets as Leaders," *Poetry,* XLVIII (September, 1936), 330-34.
"Twenty-Four Years," *Poetry,* XLIX (October, 1936), 30-33.

140HARRIETMONROE

B. *Primary Materials by Harriet Monroe's Contemporaries, Associates, Contributors*

1. Books

POUND, EZRA. *The Letters of Ezra Pound: 1907-1941.* Ed. D. D. Paige. New York: Harcourt, Brace and Company, 1950. Collection of Pound's personal letters; includes many letters to Harriet Monroe at the inception of *Poetry*.

TIETJENS, EUNICE. *The World at My Shoulder.* New York: Macmillan Company, 1938. The personal story of Miss Tietjens, a young poet and an early associate editor of *Poetry*.

2. Articles

DILLON, GEORGE. "The Traveler," *Poetry*, XLIX (December, 1936), 145-46.

FLETCHER, JOHN GOULD. "A Poet's Declaration of Rights," *Poetry*, VII (November, 1915), 88-89.

FLINT, F. S. "Imagisme," *Poetry*, I (March, 1913), 198-200.

HAGEDORN, HERMANN. "As to Preaching," *Poetry*, II (July, 1913), 142-44.

HENDERSON, ALICE CORBIN. "A Perfect Return," *Poetry*, I (December, 1912), 67-91.

————. "Too Far From Paris," *Poetry*, IV (June, 1914), 105-11.

————. "The Rejection Slip," *Poetry*, VIII (July, 1916), 197-99.

————. "Correspondences," *Poetry*, VIII (August, 1916), 254-55.

————. "Of Editors and Poets," *Poetry*, VIII (September, 1916), 308.

————. "A Jitney-Bus Among Masterpieces," *Poetry*, IX (October, 1916), 39-41.

————. "Lazy Criticism," *Poetry*, IX (December, 1916), 144-49.

————. "The Great Adventure," *Poetry*, X (March, 1917), 316-19.

————. "American Verse and English Critics," *Poetry*, XI (January, 1918), 207-12.

————. "Our Contributors," *Poetry*, XII (May, 1918), 94-96.

————. "Mannerisms of Free Verse," *Poetry*, XIV (May, 1919), 95-98.

NORTH, JESSICA NELSON. "The Late Rebellion," *Poetry*, XXII (June, 1923), 153-56.

POUND, EZRA. "Status Rerum," *Poetry*, I (January, 1913), 123-27.

————. "A Few Don'ts by an Imagiste," *Poetry*, I (March, 1913), 200-206.

————. "The Tradition," *Poetry*, III (January, 1914), 137-41.

————. "The Audience," *Poetry*, V (October, 1914), 29-30.

————. "The Renaissance," *Poetry*, VI (May, 1915), 84-91.

——. "Literary Prizes," *Poetry,* VII (March, 1916), 304-5.

——. "Status Rerum—The Second," *Poetry,* VIII (April, 1916), 38-43.

——. "This Constant Preaching to the Mob," *Poetry,* VIII (June, 1916), 144-45.

——. "Things to Be Done," *Poetry,* IX (March, 1917), 312-14.

——. "Thames Morasses," *Poetry,* XVII (March, 1921), 325-29.

——. "Mr. Pound on Prizes," *Poetry,* XXXI (December, 1927), 155-59.

——. "This Subsidy Business," *Poetry,* XXXV (January, 1930), 212-14.

——. "Manifesto," *Poetry,* XLI (October, 1932), 40-43

TIETJENS, EUNICE. "A Postscript to the Foregoing," *Poetry,* XV (March, 1920), 326-27.

——. "A Plea for a Revaluation of the Trite," *Poetry,* XXII (September, 1923), 322-25.

——. "The Cuckoo School of Criticism," *Poetry,* XLVI (May, 1935), 96-99.

WYATT, EDITH. "On the Reading of Poetry," *Poetry,* I (October, 1912), 22-25.

——. "Poetry and Criticism," *Poetry,* IV (September, 1914), 234-37.

ZABEL, MORTON D. "The Aristocrates," *Poetry,* XXXIV (Spring, 1929), 37-41.

——. "Cattle in the Garden," *Poetry,* XXXVIII (August, 1931), 268-76.

——. "Titans, Tea-Hounds, Rasslers, and Reviewers," *Poetry,* XLI (March, 1933), 326-31.

——. "Harriet Monroe: 1860-1936," *Poetry,* XLIX (November, 1936), 85-93.

——. "A Statement," *Poetry,* XLIX (December, 1936), 161-65.

SECONDARY SOURCES

1. Books

AIKEN, CONRAD. *Scepticism: Notes on Contemporary Poetry.* New York: A. A. Knopf, 1919. Comments of disenchantment with *Poetry* by one of its severest critics.

ANDERSON, MARGARET. *My Thirty Years' War: An Autobiography.* New York: Covici, Friede, 1930. Personal history of *The Little Review* by its founder-editor.

BOGAN, LOUISE. *The Achievement of American Poetry: 1900-1950.* Chicago: Henry Regnery Company, 1951. Brief survey of the movement of modern American poetry.

BROOKS, CLEANTH. *The Hidden God: Studies in Hemingway, Faulkner, Yeats, Eliot, and Warren.* New Haven: Yale University Press, 1963. Selective essays on the theological implications in modern literature.

————. *Modern Poetry and the Tradition.* New York: Oxford University Press, 1965. Critical analyses in the problems of form, language, and meaning of twentieth-century poetry.

COFFMAN, STANLEY K. *Imagism: A Chapter for the History of Modern Poetry.* Norman: University of Oklahoma Press, 1951. Exploration into the origins, doctrines, and personalities of the Imagist movement.

COLLINS, A. S. *English Literature of the Twentieth Century.* Fourth Edition. London: University Tutorial Press, 1960. Survey study of contemporary British literature; excellent reference of names, titles, and dates.

COLUM, MARY. *Life and the Dream.* New York: Doubleday and Company, 1947. Perceptive personal account of the aspirations of a young poetess in the time of *Poetry*'s early years.

COWLEY, MALCOLM, ed. *After the Genteel Tradition: American Writers 1910-1930.* Carbondale: Southern Illinois University Press, 1964. Very full study of the ideals and writers who revolted against the polite artificiality of the "genteel" tradition.

DAICHES, DAVID. *Poetry and the Modern World.* Chicago: University of Chicago Press, 1948. Perceptive critical investigation of modern poetry as reflective of the philosophical turmoil of the twentieth century.

DUFFEY, BERNARD. *The Chicago Renaissance in American Letters: A Critical History.* Ann Arbor: Michigan State University Press, 1956. Specialized history of the many major and minor literary figures who contributed to the birth of Chicago as a center of creative literature.

EASTMAN, MAX. *The Literary Mind.* New York: Charles Scribner's Sons, 1931. Personal biography of one critic's struggle to evolve a critical theory for the new poetry.

ELIOT, T. S. *Selected Essays.* Third Edition. London: Faber and Faber, 1951. Collection of Eliot's famous essays which set the direction and tone of modern criticism.

FLETCHER, JOHN GOULD. *Life Is My Song.* New York: Farrar and Rinehart, 1937. Personal reminiscence of the Chicago literary scene at the turn of the century.

FOSTER, RICHARD. *The New Romantics: A Reappraisal of the New Criticism.* Bloomington: Indiana University Press, 1962. Recent assessment of the modern changes and problems in contemporary critical theory.

GOODWIN, K. L. *The Influence of Ezra Pound.* New York: Oxford University Press, 1966. Extensive account of Ezra Pound's role in discovering and fostering new poetic talents.

GREGORY, HORACE. *Amy Lowell: Portrait of the Poet in Her Time.* New York: T. Nelson, 1958. Scholarly study of the life and times of Amy Lowell. Develops fully Miss Lowell's relationship with Harriet Monroe.

GREGORY, HORACE and MARYA ZATURENSKA. *A History of American Poetry: 1900-1940.* New York: Harcourt, Brace and Company, 1942. Comprehensive history of the forces and nature of modern American poetry.

HALPER, ALBERT. *This Is Chicago.* New York: Holt and Company, 1952. Collection of essays on the emerging developments of Chicago, both as a great industrial center and as a literary focal point in modern letters.

HANSEN, HARRY. *Midwest Portraits: A Book of Memories and Friendships.* New York: Harcourt, Brace and Company, 1923. Biographic sketches of Chicago personalities prominent in the local art world in the early twentieth century.

HOFFMAN, FREDERICK J., ed. *Perspectives on Modern Literature.* Evanston: Row, Peterson, 1962. Collection of essays exploring various facets of modern poetry as it changed through the early decades of this century.

HOFFMAN, FREDERICK J., CHARLES ALLEN, and CAROLYN ULRICH. *The Little Magazine.* Princeton: Princeton University Press, 1946. Complete history of the inception and progress of the many major "little magazines" in America; recounts their place and function in the progress of modern literature.

————. *The Twenties: American Writing in the Postwar Decade.* New York: Viking Press, 1955. A special social, biographic, and literary history of the temper of the American 1920's.

HOUGH, GRAHAM. "Reflections on a Literary Revolution," *Image and Experience.* Lincoln: University of Nebraska Press, 1960. Pp. 3-83. Very comprehensive assessment of the modern movement in literature. The author defines the basic premises and directions of the new literature and finds it generally "spiritually dispossessed." His critical perspective is Arnoldian in the extreme.

HYMAN, STANLEY EDGAR. *Poetry and Criticism: Four Revolutions in Literary Taste.* New York: Atheneum, 1961. Highly theoretical study in which the author examines the diverse foundations and changes of literary taste in modern poetry and criticism.

JONES, HOWARD MUMFORD. *The Bright Medusa.* Urbana: The University of Illinois Press, 1952. Series of lectures first delivered

in March, 1952; an examination of the relation of the arts and
the culture which supports them.

KINDILIEN, CARLIN T. *American Poetry in the Eighteen Nineties.*
Providence: Brown University Press, 1956. Study of American
verse, 1890-99; contains useful commentary on many minor poets.

LINDSAY, VACHEL. *The Congo and Other Poems.* Introduction by
Harriet Monroe. New York: Macmillan Company, 1914. An
early collection of Lindsay's most famous poems, many of which
were initially published in *Poetry.*

LOWELL, AMY. *Tendencies in American Poetry.* Boston: Houghton
Mifflin Company, 1928. Miss Lowell's version of the Imagist
movement; does not accord Pound an important place in its
formation.

MUMFORD, LEWIS. *Roots of Contemporary American Architecture.*
New York: Reinhold, 1952. Discussion of the diverse styles of
American architecture. Excellent commentary on the Columbia
Exposition.

O'CONNOR, WILLIAM VAN. *An Age of Criticism: 1900-1950.* Chicago:
Henry Regnery Company, 1952. Analysis of the changing critical
theories in American poetry.

SEYMOUR, RALPH F. *Some Went This Way.* Chicago: R. F. Seymour,
1945. Personal sketches of some of the people who helped found
Poetry, including a portrait of Harriet Monroe.

SMITH, ALSON. *Chicago's Left Bank.* Chicago: Henry Regnery Com-
pany, 1953. Journalistic account of the people and places in-
volved in the Chicago renascence: interesting contrast portraits
of Harriet Monroe and Margaret Anderson.

STARRETT, VINCENT. *Born in a Bookshop: Chapters from the Chicago
Renascence.* Norman: University of Oklahoma Press, 1965. Short
personal account of people and places who contributed to the
Chicago renascence.

SWINNERTON, FRANK. *The Georgian Literary Scene: 1910-1935.* New
York: Farrar and Rinehart, 1951. Literary history which explores
for British poetry the same time span of *Poetry* on the Ameri-
can scene.

WHITTEMORE, REED. *Little Magazines.* University of Minnesota Pam-
phlets on American Writers. Minneapolis: University of Minnesota
Press, 1963. Brief history of the place and importance of the
"little magazine" as an outlet for noncommercial and innovative
writing. Concentrates attention on a few typical little magazines,
including *Poetry.*

ZABEL, MORTON DAUWEN, ed. *Literary Opinion in America.* Rev. ed.
New York: Harper and Brothers, 1951. Diverse collection of

essays on the changing literary opinion in America; includes some excellent insights into the place of *Poetry*.

ZIFF, LARZER. *The American 1890's*. New York: Viking Press, 1966. Intensive study of the literature of the 1890's, with a special concentration on Chicago figures.

2. Articles

ALLEN, CHARLES. "American Little Magazines: I. Poetry: A Magazine of Verse," *American Prefaces*, III (November, 1937), 28-32. A brief journalistic essay, recounting the high points of *Poetry's* artistic discoveries and successes under Harriet Monroe's editorship.

—————. "The Advance Guard," *Sewanee Review*, DI (July-September, 1943), 410-29. Records the crucial role of the "little magazine" in the advancement of literature; they do not exist for commercial reasons and therefore can be in "advance" of public opinion.

BOIE, MILDRED. "A Wider Audience for Poetry," *The North American Review*, CCXLV (Summer, 1938), 408-14. Review of Harriet Monroe's autobiography, with special comment on the wider audience for the poet.

COLUM, MARY. "The Stuffy Side of Experience," *The Forum*, XCIX (May, 1938), 280. Uncomplimentary review of Harriet Monroe's autobiography, *A Poet's Life*.

GREGORY, HORACE. "The Unheard of Adventure—Harriet Monroe and Poetry," *The American Scholar*, VI (Spring, 1937), 195-200. One of the few early evaluations of Harriet Monroe's editorial policies. Recounts the history of *Poetry's* success as a stable and stimulating "little magazine."

MASTERS, E. L. "The Poetry Revival in the United States," *American Mercury*, XXVI (July, 1932), 272-80. Appreciative essay on the works of Edmund Clarence Stedman and his literary associates, Stoddard, Cawein, Moody, and others.

MENCKEN, H. L. "Puritanism as a Literary Force," *A Book of Prefaces*. New York: A. A. Knopf, 1917, 197-283. Bright and engaging essay on our Puritan heritage and its continuing powers for moral and sexual hypocrisy.

PARKER, CLARA M. "The New Poetry and the Conservative American Magazine," *Texas Review*, VI (October, 1920), 44-66. Examines the inherent problems of the commercial magazine which must please a large general audience.

RICE, W. "Ezra Pound and *Poetry*," *Dial*, LIV (May 1, 1913), 370-71. Extremely harsh critical judgment of Ezra Pound as an intellectually and technically deficient poet.

ROSCOE, B. "Flint and Fire," *Saturday Review of Literature*, XVII (March, 1938), II. Brief review of Miss Monroe's autobiography, *A Poet's Life*.

SANDBURG, CARL. "The Work of Ezra Pound," *Poetry*, VII (February, 1916), 249-57.

STROBEL, MARION. "For Harriet Monroe," *Poetry*, XLIX (December, 1936), 143-45.

SUTTEN, WALTER. "Criticism and Poetry," *American Poetry*, ed. Irvin Ehrenpresis. London: Edward Arnold Publishers, 1965. Intensive study on the complementary and reciprocal relationship of the creative and critical aspects of poetry.

SWETT, MARGERY. "Free Verse Again," *Poetry*, XXV (December, 1924), 153-59.

TATE, ALLEN. "American Poetry Since 1920," *Bookman*, LVIII (January, 1929), 503-8. Discussion of the anti-intellectual nature of modern poetry. Tate asserts that there is no homogeneous body of beliefs and feelings in modern literature.

————. "Editorial Note," *Poetry*, XL (May, 1932), 90-94.

Index

147

148

Masters, Edgar Lee, 33, 35, 53, 56, 58, 82
Meynell, Alice, 26, 50
Miller, Joaquin, 35, 36
Monroe, Harriet, association with Ezra Pound, 44, 49, 62-71; autobiography, *A Poet's Life*, 16, 127-30; books, *Chosen Poems*, 118, 128; *The Columbian Ode*, 24, 25, 98-104, 111, 119, 131; *The Dance of Seasons*, 104; *The Difference and Other Poems*, 111; *John Wellborn Root*, 25-26; *The New Poetry*, 75; *The Passing Show: Five Modern Plays in Verse*, 28-29, 97-98; *Valeria and Other Poems*, 25-26, 28; *You and I*, 104-11; editorial attitudes and policies, 48-49, 51, 57-58, 60-62, 71-72, 74, 76-78, 80-82, 83-88, 88-93, 124-26; education, 18-19, 20; family, 15-17, 29; founding of *Poetry*, 31-32, 33-46; free-lance writing, 20-21, 23, 29; miscellaneous poems and plays, 21, 23, 28-29, 97, 104, 112-22; religious beliefs, 67-68; travels, 20, 21-22, 26-27, 112, 113, 128-29.
Monroe, Henry Stanton, 15, 16, 17, 20, 29
Monroe, Martha, 15, 16, 17
Moody, William Vaughn, 48, 97
Moore, Marianne, 58, 125

New Criticism, 52
North, Jessica Nelson, 74, 80, 84
Noyes, Alfred, 36

Pound, Ezra, 18, 44, 45, 46, 48, 49, 51, 52, 53, 54, 55, 56, 59, 62-71, 73, 74, 75, 78, 79, 87, 89, 91, 94, 125, 129

Rago, Henry, 73
Ransom, John Crowe, 72
Reed, John, 50
Riding, Laura, 81, 91
Riley, James Whitcomb, 35, 36, 39

Robinson, E. A., 33
Root, John Wellborn, 24, 25, 26
Ryder, Albert Pinkham, 30

Sandburg, Carl, 33, 53, 56, 58, 59, 82
Seeger, Alan, 59
Shaw, George Bernard, 27, 29, 98, 131
Snodgrass, William, 57
Spender, Stephan, 80, 124
Stedman, Edmund C., 20, 21, 22, 34, 96, 97
Stein, Gertrude, 86, 92
Sterling, George, 35, 36, 50
Stevens, Wallace, 58, 59
Stevenson, Robert Louis, 21, 26
Stoddard, R. H., 34
Sullivan, Louis, 24, 31
Sullivan, Margaret, 20
Synge, John Millington, 61

Tagore, Rabindranath, 50, 58
Tate, Allen, 79, 81, 91
Taylor, Bayard, 34, 36
Thomas, Dylan, 58
Thompson, Francis, 26

Warren, Robert Penn, 72
Watkins, Vernon, 132
Watson, William, 36
Watts-Dutton, Theodore, 26
Whistler, James McNeill, 22, 49
Whitman, Walt, 46, 59, 87, 103, 113
Whittemore, Reed, 93-95
Wilde, Oscar, 27
Williams, William Carlos, 91
Winters, Yvor, 79, 81, 91
Woolf, Virginia, 52
Wordsworth, William, 88
Wright, Frank Lloyd, 31
Wyatt, Edith, 44, 45

Yeats, William Butler, 50, 56, 57, 58, 61, 70, 87, 88, 114

Zabel, Morton Dauwen, 76, 126